THE NEW FAT CATS

A Twentieth Century Fund Paper

THE NEW FAT CATS

Members of Congress as Political Benefactors

by Ross K. Baker

P P Priority Press Publications/New York/1989

Library of Congress Cataloging-in-Publication Data
Baker, Ross K.
    The new fat cats.

    "A Twentieth Century Fund paper."
    Includes index.
    1. Campaign funds—United States. 2. Political action committees—United States. 3. United States. Congress—Elections. 4. United States. Congress—Leadership. I. Title.
JK1991.B35   1989   324.7'8'0973   89-10281
ISBN 0-87078-301-7
ISBN 0-87078-300-9 (pbk.)

Foreword

In American politics, a campaign contribution typically represented a straightforward transaction in which money flowed from those outside politics to those seeking to obtain or to remain in office. In recent years, however, members of Congress have begun to employ PACs to channel campaign contributions to fellow members—members whose support they need to achieve leadership posts or other forms of influence.

At a time when campaign finance is already under scrutiny, the advent of these "member" or "leadership" PACs is perceived by many as cause for acute concern. There are those who suspect that trickery or misrepresentation characterizes the relationship between member PACs and those who habitually contribute to them. Others fear that member PACs siphon money from the party campaign committees, further weakening the parties and decreasing political competition by providing additional support to incumbents. Finally, some fear that these new PACs will result in excessive involvement by outsiders in the affairs of Congress.

The Fund has had a long-standing interest in campaign finance. In 1967, it sponsored the independent, bipartisan Commission on Campaign Costs in the Electronic Age, which issued the report *Voters' Time*. Since then, it has published *Electing Congress: The Financial Dilemma,* the Report of the Twentieth Century Fund Task Force on Financing Congressional Campaigns, and *What Price PACS?* the Report of the Twentieth Century Fund Task Force on Political Action Committees. And earlier this spring it released *Paying for Elections: The Campaign Finance Thicket,* a Twentieth Century Fund Paper by Larry J. Sabato.

Ross Baker, professor of political science at Rutgers University, does what those responsible for these earlier examinations have done: he probes rather than accepts the conventional wisdom. After an intensive review of the way in which membership and leadership PACs actually operate, he concludes that they do not present the dangers all too often attributed to them.

He believes, however, that they present other, perhaps greater, dangers. The fragmentation of power they breed makes the job of party leaders all the more difficult—further decreasing the importance of parties in the work of Congress. Even more damaging is their effect on an already cynical public. The specter of congressmen buying votes from each other—whatever its validity—only reinforces the public's disillusionment with the system.

Marcia Bystryn, ACTING DIRECTOR
The Twentieth Century Fund
May 1989

Contents

For
Susannah and Sally

Acknowledgments

I would like to acknowledge the assistance at the earliest stages of this project of the Center for Responsive Politics and most especially of its executive director, Ellen S. Miller, and Herbert K. Schultz, project director for campaign finance. I would also like to thank Peter H. Fenn of Fenn and King Communications of Washington, D.C., who also serves as a member of the board of the Center for Responsive Politics.

Special recognition should go to Peter Lindstrom of the Floyd Group who was responsible for the retrieval, downloading, and processing of the data from the Federal Election Commission.

I would also like to thank Alan Rosenthal, director of the Eagleton Institute of Politics of Rutgers University, and Edith Saks of Eagleton for her help in the preparation of the manuscript.

Special thanks go to John Samples, program officer of the Twentieth Century Fund, who steered this project with characteristically good sense and great sensitivity, and Jane Seegal, whose skillful editing enhanced the manuscript.

Finally, I would like to thank the members and former members of Congress who agreed to be interviewed for this paper and the PAC directors whose frank and informative discussions provided the broader context for this project. In addition, special thanks to Kent C. Cooper of the Federal Election Commission.

Introduction

Today, powerful senior members of Congress and ambitious junior members have a new tool in their struggle for congressional leadership—the so-called leadership PAC. Legislative changes in the 1970s brought about a new development in campaign financing—political action committees (PACs). Leadership PACs, developed toward the end of the decade, are formed by individual members of Congress who use the funds raised by their PACS to support the campaigns of congressional colleagues and candidates for Congress. They do so in order to gain votes from members they have supported to further their own legislative or leadership aspirations. These leadership PACs are not unlike the more usual—and visible—PACs set up by special interest groups, ranging from environmentalists to individual corporations, to raise funds to donate to political candidates in the hope of winning support for their agendas.

Although their numbers are small (since 1978, only fifty such leadership PACs have been formed), their financial impact is significant (they donated $3.5 million in the 1986 elections, an average of $70,000 each). That compares with the $140 million given out in that election by 4,100 outside PACs, which gave out an average of half as much, or $34,000 each (see Appendix, Table 1). Moreover, funding provided by leadership PACs seems to have been decisive in races for such posts as

House majority whip (the number three leadership slot), Budget Committee chair, and chair of the House Democratic Caucus (leadership of the entire Democratic membership of the House).

What is more, leadership PACs are likely to increase in number. For example, David Obey, a member of Congress from Wisconsin and a longtime critic of leadership PACs, formed his own PAC, the Committee for a Progressive Congress, in 1985. Asked about his change of heart, Obey said, "You can't play touch while the other guy's playing tackle [football]."[1]

Origins

The members' PACs have sprung indirectly and primarily from reforms in the early 1970s designed to democratize the way the House of Representatives was run. Although a few reforms occurred in the Senate, the Senate hierarchy was already rather flexible, responding more to the influence of gentle persuasion. The reformers' goals were both to enhance the role of the individual legislator and expand the authority of the party leaders in Congress, to strike a balance.

Since 1910, the seniority system used for determining leadership had enabled aging autocrats from largely conservative, southern districts to hold many key chairmanships. Then, starting in 1971, House members changed the way committee chairs were chosen, allowing approval by the Democratic Caucus by secret ballot instead of a rubber-stamp, open vote. Moreover, in 1973, the Democrats voted to have members *of each committee* vote on the subcommittees' chairs and budgets. Thus, for the first time, House members had greatly increased motives to win colleagues' favor: votes for committee or subcommittee leadership posts.

In another reform, in 1972, the caucus voted to limit the number of chairmanships that any House member could hold; similar restrictions were implemented in the Senate. The number of committees and subcommittees has declined from 385 in the mid-1970s to 299 today, but the percentage of members in chairmanships has remained more or less constant. Roughly half of the 260 House Democrats and 96.3 percent of all Democratic senators hold independent power bases from which to pursue issues—and campaign contributions.[2]

In 1974, some two years after the break-in at the Democratic National Committee headquarters in the Watergate Hotel, and the subsequent cover-up by officials in the Nixon White House, an unusually large freshman class of forty-nine Democrats arrived in Congress eager to open up the House structure. Led by the reformers, the majority-party caucus in 1975 for the first time sacked three committee chairmen, a clear sign that times had changed.

While procedures in Congress were changing, so were the rules about campaign financing. As part of an effort to limit the distorting effect of individual contributions on election campaigns, changes in campaign finance law in 1974 allowed the formation of corporate political action committees. Congress also allowed any PAC to give more to each political candidate and donate a larger total than individuals could spend. Thus, while individuals now may give $1,000 per candidate in each primary or general election, with a total limit of $25,000, PACs are allowed to give $5,000 per candidate for each primary and election with no cumulative limit.

Although PACs had existed outside of Congress earlier—with 600 of them spending about $20 million on congressional races in 1974—the total number of PACs outside Congress skyrocketed after that year so that 4,268 paid out $148,085,016 in 1988. As a result, much more money is readily available for congressional campaigns.

While members of Congress had previously donated surplus funds to colleagues' campaign chests informally, the funding law changes meant that, from 1974 on, legislators could transfer more money to their colleagues or other candidates by forming their own PACs.

Effects

If the reformers were trying to find a balance between individual initiative and party cohesiveness, the actual changes, including the rise of leadership PACs, have brought a slight shift to a somewhat greater dispersal of party power. The parties' congressional, senatorial, and national committees are no longer the sole disbursers of campaign funds from within the political ranks. Members' gratitude—and commitments to vote a certain way—may thus extend to colleagues who do not necessarily follow the party orthodoxy. And it appears that members who can more easily raise funds on their own feel freer to vote independently.

For lobbyists, the system is more inefficient: there are fifty new PACs to which they may feel obliged to write checks. But from the viewpoint of the party leadership, leadership PACs may actually be an unexpected asset. For whatever reason, the leadership PACs attract donations that the parties' conventional fund-raising arms would not likely draw in. For citizens worried about the power of incumbency, leadership PACs give a larger share of their funds to challengers than do the outside PACs.

Clearly, the rise of leadership PACs over the past decade raises a number of questions that warrant careful examination. It is important that we understand the way they work, the harm and the good they can do, before we decide if they are a part of the American campaign financing system in need of reform.

Chapter 1

Afloat on a Sea of Dollars: PACs as the Paymasters of American Politics

No aspect of American politics is so roundly condemned as the way money is raised and spent for congressional elections. It is the subject of impassioned editorials in respectable newspapers, crusades by advocates of good government, and sour comments by an increasingly cynical citizenry. Nonetheless, like the weather in Charles Dudley Warner's old lament, everybody talks about it but nobody does anything about it.

Despite significant efforts at reform in recent years, little headway has been made. Reform efforts have tended to founder on two political shoals. The first is the Supreme Court's 1976 decision in *Buckley v. Valeo,* which struck down mandatory limits in the 1974 Federal Election Campaign Act on the money a candidate could spend in a federal election. The Court upheld limits on campaign contributions but determined that restrictions on candidate spending would violate the free-speech clause of the First Amendment. Inasmuch as the *Buckley* decision still stands, subsequent efforts to reform campaign financing have promoted voluntary participation in a system of financing federal elections with public funds. But in the words of one noted jurist, "The practical difficulty with the Court's constitutional analysis is that it preserves an unrestricted avenue for political spending."[1]

The second obstacle to reform is that the acknowledged alternative to unrestricted spending by candidates, public financing, has inherent problems and many vigorous opponents. One problem would be whether Congress would appropriate enough money for proper administration by the Federal Election Commission. Some oppose public funding of congressional campaigns on grounds of fiscal prudence. The argument is made that, at a time of massive structural deficits, the diversion of public money to finance the campaigns of politicians would be both bad budgetary policy and unpopular with taxpayers. The lack of enthusiasm among voters for paying for congressional elections is confirmed by the fact that only 25 percent of taxpayers check off on their IRS forms the $1 contribution to the fund for presidential candidates. The checkoff yielded $33 million for the 1988 presidential race.

In addition, critics of public financing proposals argue that such financing could perpetuate the tactical advantages of those already in office. Under the current system, incumbents generally have the advantages of enormous name recognition and much larger campaign funds. Contributors overwhelmingly favor incumbents over challengers, as do most political action committees (PACs). From January 1987 to March 1988, PAC donations showed a huge pro-incumbent bias, with 93 percent of House-race contributions and 78 percent on the Senate side going to those already in office. Although public financing could give incumbent and challenger equal funding—and thus would likely be opposed by many officeholders—it wouldn't shift the balance enough in most cases to allow an "equal" contest given the other considerable advantages of incumbency, such as large congressional staffs skilled at constituent services and superior access to the media.

Unrestricted campaign spending is defended with the argument that the costs of getting one's message across are so expensive that some substantial source of money must be available to underwrite them. Even outside the high-priced media markets of New York, Chicago, and Los Angeles, the costs of statewide campaigns are crushing because of television advertising. The costs of modern media campaigning have become so enormous that even a generous contribution by an ordinary citizen has little impact.

A campaign aide to former Florida governor Reubin Askew, who was campaigning in the 1988 Florida Democratic primary for a U.S. Senate seat, illustrated how citizen contributions are dwarfed by the costs of campaigning. At a rally in North Florida, he said,

> a hunched-over, withered dirt farmer approached the governor with a $100 check. "I want you to have this," said the man, trembling with awe. "I've supported you for years, and I'm behind you now." With a 30-second television spot in Tampa costing around $6,000, the farmer's contribution paid for about a half-second of television. I didn't have the heart to tell him.[2]

The shrinking to insignificance of the contributions of ordinary Americans is only one loss suffered by citizens as a result of the huge cost of campaigns. The other shock to the system is that House members and senators need to spend great amounts of time raising money to wage these fabulously expensive campaigns instead of conducting public business.

In May, Askew withdrew from the race, citing the amount of time he had to spend fund-raising; Askew's experience was not unusual. A poll of 114 members of the House and Senate and 115 staff members in 1987 by the Washington-based Center for Responsive Politics found that almost 30 percent of members questioned said that the demands of campaign fund-raising "significantly" cut into the time they devote to legislative work. An additional 18 percent said that the fund-raising activities had "some effect." But the diversion of legislative energies to campaign activities was even more marked in the case of those who work for members and senators. Virtually half of all staff people indicated that fund-raising was a significant diversion from their legislative work.[3]

A survey undertaken in 1983 by the Campaign Finance Task Force of the House Democratic Caucus among Democratic House members found even more dramatic evidence that fund-raising was consuming the time of legislators. That poll reported that 73 percent of respondents agreed or agreed strongly that "members' schedules are too much dictated by the need to raise campaign funds." Thus, two surveys have found that between half and three-fourths of members believe that the demands of fund-raising distort the way they conduct—or should be conducting—the public business.

Much of the time and energy spent by members of Congress seeking campaign contributions is directed toward PACs, which have become a major force in campaigns. While at least one labor PAC was created in 1943—the Congress of Industrial Organizations' PAC—as late as 1972 there were only 113 PACs.

The 1974–75 period marks the great transition in the development of PACs. Amendments by Congress to the legislation creating the Federal Election Commission (FEC) setting limits on the amount individuals could contribute to federal campaigns, and a ruling by the FEC in the SunPAC case that permitted corporations to solicit voluntary political donations from employees led to an upsurge in the number of PACs. Their numbers have soared since 1974 by an astonishing 611 percent. While individual contributors and the candidate's own resources still are the most important source of campaign income, the PACs' share of all congressional campaign receipts rose from 17 percent in 1978 to 28 percent in 1986. During the same time, the percentage of total campaign contributions from individual givers fell to 57 percent.[4]

What brought a rise in the number and influence of PACs were, paradoxically, reforms in the aftermath of the campaign finance scandals of the Nixon years over donations by wealthy individuals. So limits were set for individual contributors' donations, while PACs were allowed to give more to each candidate and more overall than individual donors.

Politics in the Age of PACs

The entity designated by the Federal Election Campaign Act as a "multicandidate political committee" and now known by all as a PAC is an intriguing political innovation. To be best understood, a PAC should be considered a political mutual fund. As the investor relies on a mutual-fund manager to invest his or her money in a variety of companies, the political contributor can give money to a PAC and have the PAC director donate the funds to a variety of candidates. Because many donors have neither the time nor knowledge to evaluate the records of more than a few candidates, it is efficient to use the PAC as an intermediary.

Someone wishing to support liberal causes gives to a liberal PAC, for example. Employees of a corporation contribute to their corporate PAC in the expectation that the PAC director will channel the money to those members of Congress whose committee jurisdiction is vital

to the well-being of the company, or to members repre-
senting states or districts where the corporation is located. Citizens wanting to advance the cause of civil
rights or the State of Israel, or to oppose abortion, can
send their checks to the appropriate PACs with the expectation that the funds will be targeted to the right
members of Congress.

The advent of PACs has done much to accelerate a
trend in which the candidate, rather than the party, is
key. Modern American politics for the past twenty-five
years has been media centered. With the decline in party
influence, politics has become candidate centered as
well. Most recently, campaigns are verging on becom-
ing PAC centered.

PACs are the major source of candidate contributions
not controlled by the political parties. Business PACs,
which have experienced the most dramatic growth in
recent years, base their giving on criteria far different
from those that would be used by a party. Business PACs
are relentlessly pro-incumbent. Party groups need to
support their candidates, whether challengers or incumbents. But if incumbents control public policy and those
incumbents happen to be Democrats, it would ill behoove
even the most ardent Republican business PAC director to deny them money. So while business may be
thought to favor Republicans, the pattern of business
PAC giving often seems to fly in the face of the old political axiom about rewarding friends and punishing ene-
mies. As one director of a business PAC described his
contribution strategy,

First, you get to everyone on Ways and Means whether
they're for you or against you. Secondly, there's a
presumption that we look seriously into giving to incumbents where we have a major facility unless the guy has
gone out of his way to urinate on us. And we give money

to guys where we have major facilities who vote against us nine times out of ten.*

Applying no standard to a contribution other than a member's incumbency and committee jurisdiction, PACs pay a form of political protection to those who make the public policy that affects their parent organizations.

PACs generally absorb money that has traditionally gone to political parties. More important, perhaps, PACs also absorb much of the energy of those who formerly worked through the parties to influence public policy. If parties with their comprehensive agendas designed to appeal to the broadest segments of the population stand at one end of the spectrum, PACs with their narrow focus tailored to appeal only to those with a special interest stand at the other. PACs have, by their very nature, a fragmenting effect on politics. They enable groups with narrow interests to contribute money to politicians who have single-issue agendas. Members of Congress are held to no overall philosophical account by most PACs. And PACs lavish on legislators the money needed to win campaigns at a time when the average House race costs almost $270,000 and the average Senate race close to $3 million.

Experts dispute the effect PACs have had on the two major political parties. Some argue that PACs have become dependent on party organizations for information as to who should receive money.[5] Others minimize the effect party officials have on who receives PAC money. They point to evidence that PACs do not look to party groups for advice about giving, but turn, instead, to colleagues running the largest and most influential political action committees.[6] In fact, the case has been made

---

* This quotation and others without separate citations are based on interviews conducted by the author during 1988.

that political parties, by directing their support to candidates who are electable regardless of their commitment to the principles of the party, are emulating the tactics of the PACs.[7]

The more money a member of Congress can attract from PACs, the more that member can be independent of the party. While relatively junior members with little influence need the money provided by the two parties' congressional and senatorial campaign committees, senior members of key committees are like monarchs on royal barges afloat on a sea of dollars. And it is this group that has taken the PAC idea one dramatic step further: the establishment of the leadership PACs.

Leadership PACs are part of the broader phenomenon of increasing autonomy for individual House members and senators—autonomy from the political party whose label they bear and from the leadership of the chamber in which they sit. The members' PACs also partly reflect societal changes of the 1960s and 1970s, in which institutions ranging from universities to voluntary organizations were forced to be more responsive to those they served.

In addition to modifying the seniority system and dispersing committee power, the congressional reformers of those two decades implemented so-called sunshine laws; they also moved to consolidate some power in the party leadership of the House.

House committee and subcommittee hearings were opened to the press in 1970; three years later, the House opened all committee sessions to the public unless the committee—in open meeting—voted to close them. The Senate, in 1975, adopted similar rules. All House floor proceedings were televised beginning in 1978, and by 1986 the Senate had followed suit.

In an attempt to counterbalance the increased independence of House members, the Democrats from 1973 to 1975 took steps to give the speaker and floor leader a major role in making committee assignments. The Ways and Means Committee was stripped of its role as the party's committee on committees, a role given to the new Steering and Policy Committee dominated by party leaders. The speaker also won the right to nominate members to the Rules Committee, subject to caucus approval. The Rules Committee determines whether legislation is voted on by the full House.

The reforms designed to centralize power in the leadership's hands have had mixed success. While a measure of party discipline has been achieved by the dominant role of the speaker in the committee assignment process and the work of the Rules Committee, party leaders have not asserted themselves strongly. Defiance of leadership—especially by the most senior members—rarely results in punishment for any but the most egregious offenses. Junior members can be blocked by the House leadership from improving their committee assignments, but committee and subcommittee chairs are, even today, rarely punished for party irregularity.

Given the current weakness of party leadership, leadership PACs represent one more possible threat to the speaker's and majority leader's abilities to build effective coalitions on important legislation.

Chapter 2

The Proto-PACs:
Member-to-Member
Contributions and the
Campaign Committees

In the eyes of the Federal Election Commission (FEC),
which enforces the regulations on campaign contributions, PACs established by House members or senators
are like those set up by unions or corporations. They are
classed together as "multicandidate political committees" qualified to give money to those seeking office.

What sets apart leadership PACs (member PACs) from
ordinary PACs is that they are often used to funnel contributions from one member of Congress to another. A
PAC's funds, moreover, can be used to finance travel for
the member who establishes it. This enables the member to attend political events throughout the country and
build a national constituency.

Actually, leadership PACs are the institutionalization
of a long-standing practice: the transfer of funds from
House members and senators who have money or access
to it to those who are politically needy and have few
sources of support. In some instances, the contributions
come from colleagues' personal funds. In other cases,

15

legislators from safe seats who have raised more money than they need share their bounty with colleagues. Establishing a PAC enables a member to give colleagues larger donations than would be allowed from the member's personal or campaign funds. In yet another category of member-to-member beneficence, a member or senator acts as a conduit—raising money from private contributors and disbursing it to candidates he or she deems worthy. An important part of this approach has been that the recipient knows who provides his or her good fortune. It was on such an approach to campaign finance that the congressional career of Lyndon B. Johnson of Texas was built.

LBJ and the 1940 Campaign: The Daddy of Fat Cats

In the 1940 congressional campaign, when it appeared that the Democrats were in danger of losing the House, an enterprising junior congressman from Texas named Lyndon B. Johnson organized an extraordinary drive to raise money from Texas oil wildcatters to benefit his Democratic colleagues. At the time, the Democratic National Committee (DNC) and the Democratic Congressional Campaign Committee (DCCC) were the principal sources of campaign funds for House Democrats. The DCCC had been established in the late nineteenth century to raise and distribute campaign funds to Democrats running for the House. Both committees were strapped for money and unable to do much for beleaguered incumbents. Johnson, working with only the flimsiest official sanction from the Roosevelt White House and Speaker Sam Rayburn, single-handedly turned what had been developing into a Democratic debacle into a gain of eight seats.[1]

What did Johnson receive for the effort? He became a power in the House. Biographer Robert Caro says,

The new power he possessed did not derive from
Roosevelt's friendship, or from Rayburn's. It did not derive from his seniority in the House, nor even—despite
the relationship that power in a democracy bears to the
votes of the electorate—to his seat in it. His power was
simply the power of money.[2]

The 1940 campaign launched Johnson on a career that
would ultimately vault him into the White House. But
it was his ability to tap great wealth and deploy it effectively among his colleagues that was to mark his
career in Congress. He pursued it later in the Senate
with Senator Robert Kerr of Oklahoma, who served until
1963, acting as his paymaster.

Johnson's practice of raising money from wealthy Texans and acting as the conduit for the contributions—
always making sure that the recipients were mindful
of the role he was playing—did not involve any of Johnson's personal or campaign funds. He was a collector of
contributions who directed the checks from outside Congress to where they were needed and, in turn, received
a kind of handling fee in the form of the gratitude of
the recipients.

Among southern members in particular there had also
grown the practice of giving one's campaign surplus to
other members. Journalist Elizabeth Drew identifies
onetime House Whip Hale Boggs of Louisiana as the
father of the practice, but its paternity is unclear. Known
as "cash on hand," this form of member-to-member donation was the informal forerunner of the leadership
PAC. Former congressman Richardson Preyer of North
Carolina recalls, "It was an effort to help people who
needed a little help. If you raised more money than you
needed to spend in your campaign, you'd give some to
a couple of other members of your delegation who were
hard up for funds. This early form of giving was not

directed to any particular purpose such as gaining control of a committee or anything of that sort. It was generally sort of good-will giving and in fairly small amounts."

A less charitable view of the phenomenon was provided by former congressman Richard Bolling of Missouri,
who recalled,

> I don't think there's any question but that the highly
> organized southern conservatives had a self-support sys-
> tem that went on on a continuous basis. You'd get a
> drunk who was an uncontrollable drunk in a commit-
> tee chairmanship and they'd take care of him in every
> way including contributions to his campaign. Now you
> couldn't prove that in a million years, but it was a mar-
> velous thing to watch.

Bolling was the force behind the use of the Democratic Study Group (DSG) to raise money for liberal
Democrats. In 1963, with the help of Adlai Stevenson,
the DSG, which had been a research and support organization, acquired a money component. As Bolling recalls,
"It was more open and more formal than what the
southern conservatives were doing" because of the institutional status of the DSG and the fact that fund-
raising and contributions were not concealed.

The effort by the liberals of the DSG was based upon
a desire to maintain or augment the ranks of those who
shared their outlook and should be distinguished from
Johnson's approach, which was based more upon idiosyn-
cratic motives. In Robert Caro's view,

> A hallmark of Johnson's career had been a lack of any
> consistent ideology or principle, in fact of any moral foun-
> dation whatsoever—a willingness to march with any ally
> who would help his personal advancement. His work
> with the congressional campaign committee brought this
> into sharper focus.[3]

It was this indifference to the political characteristics of those who received his largess that made LBJ's approach—unlike the subsequent efforts by the liberals of the DSG—the forerunner of the contemporary leadership PAC. Indeed, most of those who received campaign funds through Johnson's efforts in 1940 were northern liberals competing in swing districts. Fellow Texans and Democrats from the then-solidly Democratic South ran without opposition and needed none of Johnson's aid. The money, moreover, came from contributors who abominated the politics of those ultimately receiving their money. "He was helping New Dealers with the money of men who hated the New Deal."[4]

Johnson never deceived his stable of Texas contributors about the ultimate destination of their dollars. Deception was not necessary. They trusted Johnson to dispense the money strategically because what they expected in return was not a philosophically friendly Congress but one that could provide them with what they wanted. They wanted the tangible bounty of government: contracts, subsidies, and tax breaks for their industries. And, for these tangible gifts, the votes of grateful liberals were worth as much as those of conservatives.

Johnson became a master broker of that magical political commodity of reciprocity. Favors bestowed imply favors returned. That kind of obligation became the pivot on which his career turned. And it also set the precedent for future practitioners.

The Role of Party Campaign Committees

Johnson's activities in the 1940 campaign were never formally associated with the DCCC. Yet ideally, party campaign committees in the House and Senate should be tools of party discipline—to give funds to those members who vote faithfully with the party leadership and to be less generous with the renegades.

The use of these campaign committees to enforce party support has been sporadic because their ability to function depends on almost perfect conditions: strong party leadership, policy consensus within the party, and available money. Success also requires a campaign committee chair willing to be an aggressive fund-raiser and an active participant in elections on behalf of party candidates.

Chairmanships of these committees have devolved upon a variety of types of members. In the 1960s, Mike Kirwan, who represented an Ohio district, used the DCCC post to foster what amounted to a personal agenda. Kirwan's power base was the Appropriations Subcommittee on Public Works, and he used it along with his campaign committee chairmanship to demand deference from his colleagues. On one occasion, he was told by James Roosevelt, then a California congressman, that he would be unable to attend the next day's tribute to Kirwan's success as a fund-raiser being held in Los Angeles. Roosevelt cited a pressing commitment in Washington. "Gee, that's too bad," replied Kirwan. "Will you still be appearing before my committee next week about that river you want dredged?" Roosevelt replied that he would. "Fine," said Kirwan, who asked Roosevelt once more where he would be the following evening. Knowing he had been bested, Roosevelt replied, "Looks like I'll be at your party, Mike."[5]

But for all of Kirwan's claims on fealty from his colleagues, he was remarkably casual about dispensing funds from the DCCC: every Democrat running received $500. Kirwan, moreover, preferred to remain in Washington and oversee his powerful subcommittee rather than travel around the country assisting the campaigns of Democratic candidates. When he died in 1970, the DCCC chairmanship was assumed by Thomas P. ("Tip") O'Neill, a congressman from Massachusetts at the time, who scrapped Kirwan's policy of indiscriminate contributions in favor of a more systematic one. O'Neill, moreover, was an indefatigable traveler who stumped the country for his candidates.[6]

O'Neill was something of a pioneer in the use of polls to determine where DCCC money needed to be targeted. He also used the poll to take the first soundings on how a vote to impeach President Nixon would affect members' reelection chances.

Chairmanship of the Democratic campaign committee had not tended to be the springboard to leadership it had been among House Republicans. For example, Joseph W. Martin, Jr., of Massachusetts and Charles Halleck of Indiana had chaired the National Republican Congressional Committee (NRCC) and used their success to become speaker and floor leader, respectively.[7]

O'Neill's success as DCCC chairman certainly helped his rise up the Democratic leadership ladder and his accession to the speakership in 1976. O'Neill might not have had much flexibility in giving party money to incumbents, inasmuch as giving more money to one incumbent than to another might smack of favoritism. But O'Neill could exercise discretion with candidates for open seats. A House Democrat interviewed by political scientist Robert Peabody saw O'Neill's actions this way: "I suppose the main benefit [in being DCCC chairman] is being able to put money into or withhold it from non-incumbent races. A freshman might have difficulty overlooking a candidate for party leadership who appears to have just put $5,000 into his campaign."[8]

If the Democrats under O'Neill innovated, it was the Republicans who demonstrated that party organizations could raise impressive amounts of money. Between 1976 and 1982, for example, income for the three GOP national party organizations—the Republican National Committee and the House and Senate campaign committees—rose from $43 million to $191 million, while the Democrats' three committees moved, during the same period, in a modest range from $15 million to $29 million.[9]

Impressive as was the rise of receipts of the GOP and Democratic committees, the 1970s saw the party committees recede in importance as sources of funds for congressional candidates. In 1972, party committees accounted for 17 percent of the contributions to all House campaigns and 14 percent to all Senate contests. By 1974, only 4 percent of House campaign contributions came from party committees; in the Senate the party contribution dropped to 6 percent.[10] In absolute dollars, contributions from party groups to House and Senate candidates of both parties rose steadily between 1972 and 1984, with the three Democratic committees—the DNC, DSCC (Democratic Senatorial Campaign Committee), and DCCC—spending $66 million in 1984. But these party contributions represented a declining share of funds used in congressional campaigns.

Imperceptibly at first, but more noticeably as the 1970s progressed, the new entity known as the PAC was surging as the source of congressional campaign funds. It is one of the sad and paradoxical developments in the history of the congressional party leadership that at roughly the same time that party campaign committees were rationalizing their system of contributions and raising substantial sums for their congressional candidates, they were overtaken and surpassed by PACs—entities that negate a responsive party system.

Member-to-Member Contributions
Come Out of Hiding

One other trend bears on the development of PACs established by members of Congress: the increased openness of member-to-member contributions in battles for congressional leadership posts.

Although the practice of members giving contributions to colleagues was widespread—particularly among southerners—it was rarely spoken of and cannot be effectively documented. Bolling recalled,

> I know that a good deal of money moved around but it was not illegal to have long green. Nobody ever talked about it. Even later on in my career when I was more "in," I heard very few specific details. The reason it was legal was because there weren't any laws and a lot of it moved around in cash.

There is, however, no evidence that—until the 1970s—campaign contributions from one member to another were used directly to influence elections to leadership posts.

There was little use of money to influence internal elections because of the way leadership posts were achieved. Chairmanships devolved automatically upon the most senior committee member of the majority party, and only the speaker and floor leaders were elected by the membership. Even these elections often seemed formalistic, since elevation to leadership posts was the product of closed-door nominations by a handful of influential people.

By the mid-1970s, however, reforms had made it easier to challenge dictatorial or out-of-touch committee leaders. The subcommittees' new autonomy from their parent committees led to real contests for chairmanships. The requirement by the majority Democrats of caucus approval for all chairs of standing committees meant that the organization of all House Democrats constituted an electorate as never before.

But the changes also replaced certainty with a process that was problematical. While the strict application of the seniority principle had caused many committees to be saddled with leaders well past their peak, seniority made politicking irrelevant. The changes meant that those with leadership aspirations had to build support among other members. Thus, the race for House majority leader in 1970 saw a departure in the internal politics of leadership succession—for the first time, according to those interviewed. Democrats elected in November 1970 but not yet sworn in were lobbied extensively by contenders for the job. Arizona Congressman Morris K. Udall telephoned all newly elected Democrats on election night and sent each a copy of his book, *The Job of a Congressman*.[11]

Udall's genteel, but unsuccessful, lobbying was a harbinger of more vigorous efforts to come. As new members whose campaigns were touched by the Vietnam War and the Watergate scandal began entering Congress, they demanded responsibilities and a greater sense of participation in the life of the chamber. Committee and subcommittee leadership opportunities opened up.

Party leadership could expand less dramatically. There could be, after all, only one set of floor leaders for each party in each house as well as one House speaker. Whips, or deputy floor leaders, among House Democrats were appointed by the majority leader in consultation with the speaker. Some reformers among House Democrats began to press for an elective whip—conferring democratic legitimacy on a hitherto appointive post and affixing it as a new rung on the leadership ladder. Behind this move was the man who, more than any other, propelled House members in the direction of bankrolling colleagues to advance in the leadership.

Phillip Burton and the California Gold Rush

Every available account suggests that the late Phillip Burton was a man of rare talent, considerable energy, fierce determination, and great political astuteness. He assumed the chairmanship of the DSG in 1971 after defeating a candidate backed by influential members in the group. Burton revitalized the DSG by going beyond the core liberal group and enrolling moderates, border-state conservatives, and even some older members. The DSG chairmanship gave Burton's voice great resonance in the caucus.[12]

In 1972, after the disappearance and presumed death of Hale Boggs, O'Neill was elected to replace him as majority leader. Two highly regarded members were in line for appointment to the post of majority whip—John J. McFall and John Brademas, congressmen at the time from California and Indiana, respectively. But the entire concept of the appointive whip was challenged in November by Burton. On election night, in his capacity as DSG chair, he telephoned the newly elected Democrats urging them to support his amendment in caucus to make the job elective. What he did not say and what came out only later was that he was a candidate for whip in the event the caucus decided to alter the status of selection. Only a dramatic, last-minute speech by the new majority leader in favor of keeping the appointive whip prevented the Burton proposal from carrying. O'Neill went on to appoint McFall and Brademas as co-whips, but Burton's leadership ambitions were not laid to rest.

It was the retirement of House Speaker Carl Albert in 1976 and the certain elevation of O'Neill to the speakership that provided the next opportunity for Burton, who by then chaired the caucus. Burton had used his post as DSG chairman to help Democratic candidates and, in the recollection of one former colleague, "worked with interest groups with whom he was friendly to take care of people [and] at the same time make sure that the people who got the money gave him credit for it."

The 1976 race for majority leader in the House represented a major departure from past funding practice. In that contest, three of the four candidates gave colleagues money to secure their support.

Characteristically, Burton was first off of the starting blocks. At the Democratic National Convention in New York that year, he met with House candidates and prospective candidates to solicit their votes for leader in the event that they were elected. Congressmen Jim Wright of Texas and Bolling assisted House candidates in campaign fund-raising, while McFall seemed to rely more on the tradition of the party elevating whips to the post of floor leader.[13]

While FEC records at the time are not reliable because of inexperience with the new reporting forms, a number of those who observed the race closely say that at one point Burton began to dispense funds from his own campaign committee to colleagues. It did not take long for the practice to be detected by the others. There was no question but that Burton's contributions were tied to support for him—and the others were confronted with a decision about how to respond. An observer who was present at the time reported that Bolling's campaign manager, Gillis W. Long, then a congressman from Louisiana, pleaded with Bolling to contribute to colleagues to garner support. Bolling expressed distaste for the practice and refused to emulate Burton. Wright apparently did make contributions.

While Wright won the contest by a single vote, it was Burton who got the credit as the innovator. One member who observed the contest credited Burton with adapting to the House of Representatives a system that had been practiced for several years in California, where Jesse Unruh, assembly speaker in the 1960s, raised money, which he then dispensed to Democratic candidates.[14] Like so many other innovations from California, the system of giving campaign contributions to legislative colleagues to secure support for leadership positions or legislation was soon to be emulated elsewhere.

The first overt use of the California system introduced by Burton came in 1979. It is the event that most experts consider the first open and well-documented example of a rank-and-file member of Congress contributing money to colleagues in the expectation of support for an elective post.

Chapter 3

The Institutionalization of Mutual Aid: The Birth and Rise of Leadership PACs

At the conclusion of the 95th Congress in 1978, Florida Democrat Paul Rogers retired as chairman of the Subcommittee on Health and the Environment of the Commerce Committee, setting the stage for a contest for Rogers's successor as chairman. While House reforms had made the chairmanships of subcommittees elective, there continued to be a presumption in favor of the most senior subcommittee member of the majority party. That member was David Satterfield of Virginia, a man so conservative and out of favor with his Democratic colleagues that the Democratic Caucus refused to approve him for a chairmanship. The next Democrat in line, and the early favorite to succeed Rogers, was Richardson Preyer. Described in the *Almanac of American Politics* as having a "reputation for great integrity and sound judgement," Preyer announced for the post with the expectation of winning the chairmanship.

But two places below Preyer in seniority was California Democrat Henry A. Waxman, who had served only two terms in the House. Waxman decided to challenge Preyer for the subcommittee chairmanship. He raised the question of Preyer's impartiality on matters relating to the pharmaceutical firms under the subcommittee's jurisdiction, pointing to the fact that Preyer had inherited money that had come from a pharmaceutical firm, was hostile to the idea of national health insurance, and represented a North Carolina district that would cause him to be too friendly to tobacco interests.

Waxman expanded his campaign beyond the merits with some imaginative politicking that included getting labor lobbyists to persuade committee colleagues with large numbers of blue-collar constituents to support him. The greatest novelty introduced by Waxman, however, was that, as a very junior member, he contributed $24,000 of his own money to his colleagues on the full committee and beat Preyer by fifteen to twelve with a large number of last-minute switches in Waxman's favor. What Waxman did was perfectly legal, but it was considered presumptuous.

Only the most senior members and party leaders had ever contributed funds to colleagues. Here was an upstart who, in the eyes of many, had "bought" himself a subcommittee chairmanship. Waxman's temerity enraged House reformer and Rules Committee chairman Richard Bolling, who assailed the elevation of Waxman. House Speaker Tip O'Neill was also reported to be angry because of his own support of Preyer.

While everyone, including Preyer, considered Waxman an exceedingly able member, dismay was expressed at three aspects of his contribution strategy:

- Some were shocked by the overtness of Waxman's contributions. The critics seemed less bothered by the behind-the-scenes contributions from members to colleagues.

- Another group felt that it was presumptuous for a junior member to engage in this kind of campaigning but would have been less disturbed if it had been undertaken by someone more senior.
- The most typical objection, however, was that the contribution appeared to be part of a quid pro quo for support for the chairmanship. One of these members observed, "Traditionally, you didn't give money [to a colleague's campaign] with the intention of gaining control of a committee or subcommittee or anything of that sort. It was just general good-will giving and in fairly small amounts. The Waxman thing might have been the first time that it was focused and used as a weapon to obtain something."

Bolling reacted by saying, "What Waxman did was an institutionalization of something that I think was pernicious when it was hidden. It was clear, however, that it was going to be a precedent."

Another former member of Congress reacted even more strongly:

> Waxman denied he was doing it for the purpose of getting votes, but in my mind there wasn't much question about it. My experience with those characters from California was that they were simply anti-institutional people who were very good at taking care of themselves.

The institutionalization of which Bolling spoke was the establishment in 1978 by Waxman of a group calling itself "Friends of Henry Waxman" formed to contribute to Commerce Committee members. This was the first leadership political action committee. It was decisive to Waxman's campaign for the subcommittee chairmanship. Three years later the PAC was also a major weapon against efforts by committee chairman John

Dingell of Michigan to weaken the Clean Air Act, which was up for reauthorization in 1982.

While Waxman's innovation was not widely copied at first, the initial uses of leadership PACs illuminated both their political value and abuses associated with them. Leadership PACs loomed large in Edward J. Markey's Senate campaign in 1984, the race for House majority whip in 1986, and the contest for chair of the House Democratic Caucus in 1988.

The U.S. Committee Against Nuclear War and the National Committee for Peace in Central America

Two of the most passionately debated foreign policy issues of the early Reagan years were the proposed freeze on nuclear weapons production and the question of supporting the contra forces seeking to overthrow the Marxist government of Nicaragua.

The first of these issues was championed early by Markey, a Democrat from Malden, Massachusetts. From 1980 on, Markey lobbied his colleagues energetically for a nuclear freeze, even though his own district was heavily dependent on defense industries and Markey did not serve on any committee with jurisdiction over foreign policy or military affairs. Indeed, Markey served on the powerful Committee on Energy and Commerce—the renamed Commerce Committee, in which the Waxman coup had taken place.

A few days before the June 12, 1982, nuclear freeze rally in New York that would attract 750,000 people, Markey announced the formation of the U.S. Committee Against Nuclear War with the purpose of raising money to oppose the arms race. Markey sent out a dramatic mass mailing, the centerpiece of which was an appeal for funds, written on the letterhead of a hotel in Hiroshima located close to ground zero of the 1945 nuclear explosion.[1]

Markey's organization, superficially, bore little resemblance to that of Waxman. It was not presented as part of a campaign to vault Markey into a leadership post and involved a cause rather than the internal politics of Congress. The cause and Markey's ambitions, however, were intertwined.

The U.S. Committee Against Nuclear War was a multicandidate PAC registered with the Federal Election Commission (FEC) to raise money to support candidates. The implication was that the money would go not only to incumbents but to challengers as well. Within a year, the PAC had raised $113,000, largely through mass mailings, and had given out $8,000 to candidates—about 7 percent of receipts—a sum which, although small, was not out of line with what new PACs gave out.[2]

But as the PAC became better established and its receipts grew, the percentage of its funds given out to candidates actually fell; by 1984 it was giving out only 3 percent of what it took in. Markey was using the PAC to build up a mailing list that would enable him to reach a large number of individual contributors for his attempt to get the 1984 nomination in the race for the seat of retiring Senator Paul Tsongas.

While he did not win the nomination, Markey set up yet another PAC in 1984, targeted on another hot issue—the war in Central America. But the ratio of income to contributions for this new PAC, the National Committee for Peace in Central America, was even worse than for the "freeze" PAC. The organization gave only about 5 percent of its receipts to candidates opposed to Reagan administration policy in Central America in 1984. The money did, however, start showing up in the campaign coffers of some of Markey's colleagues on the Energy and Commerce Committee who occupied safe seats and were not known as strong opponents of administration policy in Central America. One contribution went to conservative, but influential, Jamie Whitten of Mississippi, chairman of the House Appropriations Committee.

When *Washington Monthly* reporter Steven Waldman tracked down some of the individuals who had contributed sums to Markey's two PACs in the belief that they were supporting candidates opposed to an arms race and aid to the contras, most expressed consternation that so little had been expended for that purpose. As to what may have been the real, as opposed to the ostensible, purpose of the PACs, Waldman quoted a former PAC official as saying, "There was hope at every stage that the freeze could be turned into higher office for Markey, whether it was the Senate race or a presidential race."[3]

The ethical problems underscored by the two Markey PACs are somewhat different from those raised by the Waxman effort.

Contributors to Waxman's 24th District of California PAC may have wished to support Waxman's public policy agenda but must have understood its main purpose was advancing the career of the congressman. Those who supported the two Markey PACs were encouraged to contribute to further a cause. They might have been pleased to see Markey advance to the Senate, but the appeals suggested a more altruistic motive.

Internally, however, the two PAC efforts were closely related: Waxman's contributions to colleagues were presumably designed to win their support for his elevation to the chairmanship of a subcommittee of Energy and Commerce and Markey's for possible elevation to the Senate. But even after his Senate bid failed, the money given by Markey's PAC to Energy and Commerce colleagues broadened his internal influence and made unlikely a challenge to his accession to the chairmanship of the Subcommittee on Telecommunications and Finance when chairman Timothy Wirth won election to the Senate in 1986.

The 1986 Battle for House Whip

The pioneers of the early leadership PAC movement had certain traits in common. They were all House Democrats, which is not surprising given the quarter-century hold by that party in the chamber. They were also liberal Democrats; Burton, Waxman, and Markey all scored about 95 percent in ratings by Americans for Democratic Action. Two of the pioneers—Burton and Waxman—came out of the California political wars. All were able, ambitious, and energetic. All—especially the Californians—came from safe congressional seats. The safety of the California seats was the legacy of Burton, who in 1980 pushed a redistricting bill through the California Assembly, giving the Democrats a durable majority of twenty-seven to eighteen over Republicans in that state's House delegation.

Somewhat less liberal than Waxman and Burton but every bit as able and ambitious was Tony Coelho of Merced, California.

When Thomas Foley of Washington State became majority leader, Coelho sought the vacated post of majority whip with two conspicuous advantages. The first was his membership in the powerful California Democratic delegation, with its long experience in fund-raising. The second was his successful tenure as chairman of the Democratic Congressional Campaign Committee, which he "turned into a campaign money machine to which countless House Democrats [were] indebted."[4] Coelho had also succeeded where Burton had failed: he got a revision in the caucus rules that made the whip post elective.

Coelho's main competitor was Charles B. Rangel of New York, who had played the key role of intermediary between the House Democratic leadership and the Black Caucus. Also contending for the post was W. G. (Bill) Hefner of North Carolina.

An astute and popular member, Rangel enjoyed the

favor of the speaker and the solid backing of the two dozen Black Caucus members. He also had an argument in his favor: if Coelho were to become whip, all three of the party's top leaders in the House would be from the West.

There was one weapon in Coelho's arsenal that Rangel did not have and was uncertain whether he wanted to wield: a leadership PAC. Coelho had established the Valley Education Fund in anticipation of the race, but Rangel resisted setting up a PAC. "It was something that I personally and politically opposed," Rangel said. "I told all of my people that I would go into any district, campaign for anybody. . . . But, for God's sake, don't throw me into the money raising market."[5]

As the race picked up steam during the summer of 1986, Rangel buttonholed members for their support but vowed not to "out-Coelho Coelho." Rationalizing his refusal to establish a leadership PAC, Rangel mused, "If I give somebody $1,000, have I really given him anything to get his attention?" He raised the question of whether such contributions might not be construed as vote buying: "If I give [colleagues] $1,000, do I embarrass them; do they think they have some kind of obligation to vote for me?"[6]

Rangel may have protested too vigorously, for when he finally decided to establish his own leadership PAC, the Committee for the 100th Congress, he lost the high ground on the PAC issue. As a staff observer of the whip contest recalled, "By setting up his own PAC, Rangel made the fatal mistake of fighting for whip on Tony Coelho's turf. On that turf Coelho is unassailable."

Coelho contributed to 245 Democratic House campaigns plus a half-dozen Senate contests. His minimum contribution was $500 and went up to $5,000 in more than thirty instances. By contrast, Rangel was able to make contributions to only about one hundred candidates, and generally in smaller amounts. In all, Coelho's PAC disbursed almost $570,000 to House candidates, and Rangel gave out $225,000.

When the Democratic Caucus convened in December 1986, Coelho won the whip post handily, but some were dismayed by the role played by campaign contributions to colleagues. In urging the election of Hefner, Congressman Ed Jenkins of Georgia was reported to have told the caucus that the best whip was not necessarily the best fund-raiser. Jenkins's comment was a minority opinion that was to become even fainter as the leadership PAC became attractive to some of its most vocal critics.

The value of the leadership PAC or less formal contributions to the campaigns of colleagues had become an established procedure in the quest for a prestige post in the House. By 1987, the process had become increasingly open; still, no claimant for a leadership post had asked outside contributors for money specifically to get colleague support. That taboo was removed in 1988, when Richard Gephardt of Missouri relinquished the post of chairman of the House Democratic Caucus.

Carnations, Cosby, and Cash: The 1988 Contest for Democratic Caucus Chair

Contributions of cash on hand rather than money raised through a formally established PAC figured prominently in the 1984 campaign of William H. Gray III for chairmanship of the House Budget Committee. In prevailing over two competitors for the prestigious post, Gray gave away about $27,000 to seventy-five Democratic challengers and incumbents, forty-six of whom won their elections and were able to vote in the caucus for Budget Committee chair. The victory also gave Gray a highly visible post that helped him to boost his own campaign contributions from $200,000 to more than

$660,000 in two years. This enabled him to be even more generous with campaign contributions to Democratic candidates in 1986.[7]

Because chairs of the Budget Committee are limited by House rules to two terms, Gray's tenure would end with the beginning of the 101st Congress in 1989. Gray announced for the caucus chairmanship in the fall of 1987 at roughly the same time as did caucus vice-chair Mary Rose Oakar of Ohio and Mike Synar of Oklahoma. Both Gray and Oakar claimed to be close to a majority as early as November 1987, but such claims were dismissed as campaign hyperbole. The active phase of Gray's campaign could not even get under way until the budget resolution was adopted by the House. And while Gray had already circulated petitions, one of his staff assistants vowed that his boss "would use other campaign tactics."[8]

The contest came out into the open in early February 1988 at the Democratic Issues Conference at White Sulphur Springs, West Virginia. Since she was filling in for Gephardt, who was off campaigning for the Democratic presidential nomination, Oakar identified herself as "acting chair" of the caucus and distributed carnations to her colleagues. Gray brought entertainer Bill Cosby to the meeting. Synar danced with the wives of his colleagues, saying, "If I can't get to the members, I get their families to say nice things about me."[9]

The most significant inducements for support, however, were not carnations, Cosby, or dances, but cash from Gray's campaign coffers. In 1987 and the first three months of 1988, Gray made contributions totaling $35,750. An aide to Oakar said she had given funds to five other candidates "at the request of the Democratic leadership" but intended to make no other contributions. Synar said he made no contributions to colleagues.[10]

Gray's methods became even more blatant when he

courted colleagues with contributions on February 23, 1988, at a dinner at Washington's opulent Occidental Restaurant; there, Gray gave $1,000 each to ten Pennsylvania colleagues. In his invitation Gray spoke of having been "very fortunate during this election cycle" and "wanting to spread this good fortune around."[11]

Some of Gray's colleagues saw the Occidental dinner as a kind of Belshazzar's feast. One was quoted as saying, "This is the most outrageous, obvious pandering I have ever seen." More whimsically, another member quipped, "In all my years up here, I've never seen anything like it. I hope he invites me to dinner soon."[12]

If there was muttering about the dinner at the Occidental, members expressed disbelief at the next turn taken by the Gray campaign. Gray established a leadership PAC, the Committee for Democratic Opportunity, and sent out a letter to a mailing list consisting of supporters of former Pennsylvania congressman Bob Edgar. Citing the need for funds to "pursue this new challenge," Gray requested "a check for $500 to $1,000 so that I can begin to build the active support within [sic] the Democratic members of Congress to win this key leadership position."[13]

Gray was also reported to have convened a breakfast meeting at a Washington restaurant in which he asked lobbyists to contact House Democrats to urge them to support him in the caucus race. This technique was also employed by Waxman in 1979, but much more informally. Indeed, it is not at all unusual to involve outsiders in attempting to persuade colleagues to support legislation, but involvement by outsiders in leadership contests is somewhat more unusual.

When one of Gray's rivals, Synar, was asked his reaction to the employment of lobbyists for campaigning, he replied, "I'm not giving money away and I'm not using lobbyists. I'm going member-to-member because this is a very personal race."[14]

The example of Gray illustrates how members can influence their colleagues without going through the formality of setting up a PAC. Gray ultimately did establish one. Nonetheless, one can achieve considerable influence without a leadership PAC.

Even if much influence can be achieved through the use of cash on hand from members' campaign committees, PACs seem to offer members a kind of prestige. To have a PAC is, for some, a mark of their sovereignty in a Congress whose 535 members act increasingly like independent entrepreneurs.

While the early years of member and leadership PACs were dominated by liberal House Democrats, more recent years—1982-86—have seen the rise of these organizations among Senate Republicans. A number of the larger PACs set up during this period were by Republican senators such as Howard Baker of Tennessee and Bob Dole of Kansas; Baker, who retired from the Senate in 1986, and Dole, who succeeded him as Republican floor leader, sought their party's presidential nomination. More recently, however, House members and senators of all parties and ideological stripes have established PACs (see Appendix, Table 1).

While the leadership PACs currently registered with the Federal Election Commission represent only a tenth of the membership of both chambers, the dynamic identified by Senator Daniel Patrick Moynihan of New York as "the iron law of emulation" will certainly convince many more members that they must have their own PACs to be full-fledged players in Congress (see Appendix, Table 2).

Chapter 4

What's Wrong with Leadership PACs and What Can Be Done about Them?

The question remains whether leadership PACs are harming Congress or the political process.

Do Leadership PACs (and Colleague Contributions) Weaken the Party Leadership of Congress?

When Lyndon Johnson or other chairs of the DCCC or the DSG gave money to House members it was as part of the party apparatus. No one would say that Johnson or Mike Kirwan or Tip O'Neill was ignorant of the possibilities of personal advancement that come when you help your colleagues. On the Senate side, George Mitchell of Maine, who chaired the Democratic Senatorial Campaign Committee from 1985 to 1986 and did not have his own PAC, was elected majority leader in November 1988. Nonetheless, money raised by party or party-affiliated groups strengthens party leadership and its ability to build cohesion and party discipline.

The argument could be made that a contribution to a fellow partisan will bolster the party's strength in the chamber. While that is correct, the recipient's obligation flows not to the party's leaders but to the individual who gave the money.

A prominent Washington lobbyist and contributor to PACs expressed concern that leadership PACs were contributing to a fragmentation of the party leadership of Congress:

> If leadership PACs were just confined to the leadership, I wouldn't have a problem with them. What bothers me is when they're put together by nonleadership people. It tends to undermine the party structure and leadership system. People establish independent power bases and I think there's already been too much diffusion of power in Congress.

A PAC director for a major industrial firm expressed a similar view of leadership PACs set up by rank-and-file members:

> Party campaign committees provide some level of flexibility for the chosen leaders of the party to funnel money to candidates in a way that's in the best interests of the party as a whole. But when you set up a PAC just to curry favor with members so that you can get elected to something or get their vote for your amendment, I find that more difficult to justify. And when you get to those bit players who just want to set themselves up as fat cats, I think there is absolutely no justification for that.

Not all lobbyists and PAC directors perceive institutional harm from leadership PACs or colleague contributions. Indeed, they prefer not to give to the Democratic and Republican House and Senate campaign committees or party leaders because, as the director of a large corporate PAC said, you spend an awful lot of time and money courting these leadership guys and you really get next to nothing because those guys are out of the *legislative* loop. Most of the things that lobbyists do are small, little things for your company or union or whatever. And the Speaker can't help you on that. And Tom Foley [the majority leader] can't help you on that. And Tony Coelho [the majority whip] can't help you on that. And you're playing a sucker's game if you walk around town thinking you're Jim Wright's best friend because you gave money to his campaign or his PAC. He's playing on a higher field. You give to the guys at the subcommittee level who do that piddly little stuff that keeps you in business.

From the point of view of a lobbyist or PAC director, the biggest bang for the buck comes from giving not to a member of the leadership but to a member of the rank and file who is strategically placed to affect the issue that concerns those contributors. This reasoning, however, does not lead potential contributors to conclude that party leaders' PACs ought to be cut off from campaign donations. It does seem to lead them to conclude that, if the back-bench member who is critical to their interests sets up a PAC, they must contribute to it.

Thus, while many PACs outside Congress do not give to other PACs—to avoid supporting the competition and diluting their own impact—many *are* donating to member PACs.

Some outside contributors in the PAC community and among lobbyists care deeply about what they see as the institutional damage done by the proliferation of leadership PACs. One lobbyist proposed the abolition of all PACs except those set up by the party leaders on the ground that "if you care about the vitality of the party in Congress, the only contribution you ought to make is to the [Democratic and Republican] campaign committees and all the fund-raising ought to be focused on that."

But if the establishment of PACs by members then fragments contributions and diverts money from party organizations or leaders to ambitious rank-and-file members, are the contributions of leaders and members necessarily at odds?

Leaders and party campaign organizations give, essentially, to the same people as do member PACs. Indeed, member PACs may be largely compatible with those of leadership if the goals of both are to elect as many of their party's candidates as possible.[1]

But the distribution of money to candidates via member PACs rather than through the party campaign organizations is an inefficient engine of party policy. The fact that the contributions may reach the same people does not mean the results will be the same. In fact, the contribution from the leadership PAC would seem to be a more personalized gesture toward a candidate than one that comes from the campaign committee. The result, in the recipient's view, could be a less profound feeling of gratitude toward his or her party benefactor—in the case of the DCCC—than to the individual colleague. This would diminish the impact of leadership contributions with a potential attendant loss of a key element of leadership influence with members.

An advantage enjoyed by the member—as opposed to party committees—who contributes to a colleague's campaign is that the goals of the donating colleague are more obvious and typically more limited than those of the party. When a member receives a contribution from a colleague seeking support for a leadership post or for legislation, that obligation is usually discharged with the casting of a single vote. When party leaders give money, there may be a broader set of expectations that the recipient will be generally supportive of party goals. The obligation, accordingly, may be perceived as more long term.

Even Tony Coelho, a former chairman of the Democratic Congressional Campaign Committee, recognized that recipients of money from his PAC were more likely to be impressed with that contribution than they would be with funds he distributed from the DCCC. "The people you just give [campaign committee] money to don't appreciate it because they think that's what you are supposed to do anyway . . . [and] if you do your job right, you say no to a lot of people."[2]

Do Leadership PACs and Colleague Contributions Deceive Individual Outside Contributors?

The problem of who is the ultimate recipient of a contribution to a multicandidate PAC is one that affects ordinary citizens and large givers in different ways.

Mailings for the two PACs set up by Edward Markey likely led contributors to expect their money to fund pro-freeze and anti-contra candidates. When that money found its way into the hands of those whose principal claim to being deserving was their membership on committees that were useful to the internal political needs of Markey, donors expressed understandable disappointment. If they had wanted to contribute to Jamie Whitten —an unlikely decision in light of their liberal policy goals—they could have done so and did not need Markey as an intermediary. To be sure, citizen contributors could have researched the records of those in Congress to learn who shared their views on foreign policy, but Markey was saying that he would do the job for them. That is a major appeal of any PAC.

From the perspective of an ordinary citizen who wants to maximize the effect on a given policy of his or her contribution, giving to a leadership PAC is probably in-

efficient and possibly self-defeating. Giving to an individual whose position is supported by the donor can
be a more rational move, although—here too—there is
no guarantee that those funds will not be used as cash
on hand to favor colleagues whose views the contributor would oppose strongly.

From a different perspective, lobbyists and PAC directors outside of Congress seem divided on the question
of the ultimate destination of a contribution given to
a member PAC. One director of a PAC for a major industrial firm said flatly:

> We want to give directly. If this PAC is going to support
> Tom Petri [a Republican from Wisconsin], we want that
> to be a direct donation from [our firm's] employees. We
> don't want it to be a contribution through Bill Frenzel
> or Duncan Hunter [Republicans from Minnesota and
> California, respectively].

Most major givers seem unconcerned about the final
resting place of their contributions. The director of a
trade association's PAC said:

> You give money to the Bob Dole PAC not because you
> give a damn really where the money ends up. You give
> it to please Dole. And you don't give money to the DCCC
> because you hope the Democrats run Congress forever—
> God knows my members don't feel that way—but because
> Beryl Anthony [the DCCC chairman from Arkansas]
> asked you for it and you want to please him.

The chief lobbyist for a broadcasting company agreed:

> These leadership PACs solicit from some pretty sophisti-
> cated people. It's not [as if the PAC were] raising money

from the public for an environmental group that turns
out to be murdering harp seals. Ordinary Joes . . . might
have reason to be concerned as to where the money winds
up. I don't give to a multicandidate PAC with the expectation that I can direct the expenditure.

Most professional donors believe that contributions are
made to please the original recipient, and whatever hap-
pens down the line cannot be controlled; their views are
clearly tinged with fatalism:

I give money to damn near a hundred guys in a two-year
cycle. I guess I'm trusting them. I don't have the right
to ask what they do with it.

Lobbyists and PAC directors trust that the immedi-
ate recipient will put the money to whatever purpose
is deemed politically useful, even if some of the ultimate
recipients would not be at the top of a list of members
meriting contributions directly. The evidence does,
however, suggest that the contributors and recipients of
member-PAC money usually resemble each other
philosophically.

Do Leadership PACs Give Outsiders Added Impact on the Choice of Congressional Leaders?

Another concern is that leadership PACs intensify involvement by those outside Congress in the selection of
congressional leaders and give outsiders influence on
the choice of party leaders and committee personnel.

The influence exerted by lobbyists on the legislative
activities of Congress is long-standing and constitution-
ally sanctioned. The involvement by lobbyists in the
selection of leaders and committee personnel is more recent. It is a practice that has been advanced by the con-

"I see nothing wrong with accepting money from someone as long as he understands that you can't be trusted to deliver what you promise!"

tributions of outsiders to the PACs of their favorite candidates for leadership posts.

Enlisting the services of interest groups is a part of what political scientist Nelson Polsby refers to as the outside strategy for gaining a leadership post. Unlike the inside strategy of treating an election to a leadership post as a "family matter," the outside strategy uses the press and friendly lobbyists.[3]

The leadership contest between Henry Waxman and Richardson Preyer in 1979 saw, in addition to the use of contributions to colleagues, a comprehensive outside strategy that involved activating individuals who could influence a House member to vote for Waxman. One lobbyist who was enlisted in the Waxman campaign believed that Waxman, who was considered an able candidate, used an outside strategy so skillful that he could have won without giving any money to the committee Democrats:

> Henry ran a hell of a sophisticated campaign. He found out who were the principal supporters of guys on the committee back in their districts—guys who might prefer Waxman over Preyer. Doug Walgren of Pennsylvania got a call from one of his principal fund-raisers in Pittsburgh and he says, "Doug, we think that Henry Waxman is the kind of guy who should be in leadership and run the subcommittee."

It is interesting that the indignation greeting Waxman's donations to his colleagues did not greet his discreet use of outsiders such as lobbyists and district supporters of colleagues to urge those members to support Waxman. It is also noteworthy that when William Gray appealed openly for lobbyist support in 1988 for his successful bid to head the Democratic Caucus he was roundly criticized in the press. Yet the dismay that greeted Gray's call for lobbyist support likely was a reaction not to the practice but to the public nature of that appeal.

The more extensive involvement of outsiders in what used to be dealt with member to member is now common. And whether contributions to the PACs or personal campaign funds of members are involved, the very nature of interest-group politics makes it virtually certain that the resources of outsiders will be tapped in any important future contest for institutional, party, or committee leadership.

While it is impractical to ban outside involvement in congressional leadership contests, the use of contributions from outsiders to garner support for a leadership post raises questions of propriety and conflict of interest. Just as lobbyists may feel compelled to support any sitting member with influence over legislation they are worried about, they similarly may be pressured to fund the candidate with the inside track for a relevant leadership post.

For example, much of the money raised by Waxman in the 1979 leadership contest came from companies in the health industry with an obvious stake in who chairs the health subcommittee. The existence of member PACs and member-to-member contributions has little influence on the disposition of outsiders to involve themselves in congressional leadership races; they are involved in important ways other than contributing money anyway.

But in their attempts to buy further access and influence, are leadership PACs mimicking outside PACs and thus further reinforcing incumbency and the status quo? Outside PACs generally consider support for an incumbent—however hostile—to be more cost-effective than funding even the most promising challenger, given the high rate of incumbent success: 99 percent in the House and 84 percent in the Senate in 1988.

Do Leadership PACs Protect Incumbents?

Campaign finance reformer Philip M. Stern cites three undesirable results of the pro-incumbent bias of PACs in general.

- They tend to freeze out quality congressional challengers who know that only incumbents can be sure of getting the money needed to campaign.
- This deterrent to challengers limits voters' choice of candidates and of policy alternatives.
- Incumbents' superior access to money protects incompetent or even dishonest officeholders from challenge.[1]

The pattern of contributions by these PACs is biased heavily in favor of incumbents. Congressional data show that more than 84 percent of all—outside and leadership—PAC money goes to incumbents. In 1986, 68.8 percent of all PAC money went to incumbents, but it has been unusual for less than 70 percent of all PAC money in a given cycle to go to them. Political scientist Frank Sorauf identifies this pattern as part of an overall "pragmatic strategy" that "reflects the goal of pursuing and maintaining legislative access, of coordinating PAC contributions with the legislative goals of the parent organization . . . and above all, of not offending powerful incumbents by supporting their opponents."[5]

The pattern of contributions by leadership PACs appears to differ from that of outside PACs in some important respects, and is, in general, less pro-incumbent than are the patterns evident in the contributions of ordinary PACs.

The incumbents most favored by outside PACs are House Democrats. In the 1984 cycle, 82 percent of contributions to House Democrats by outside PACs went to incumbents. In the same year, the share of total contributions to House Democrats that leadership PACs gave to incumbents was smaller, about 64.7 percent. In 1986 and 1988, outside PACs gave 75 percent and 87.5 percent of all House Democratic money to incumbents. In the same two cycles, leadership PACs' shares ran only 48.5 percent and 55.4 percent, respectively (see Appendix, Table 3).

The incumbents least favored by leadership PACs have been Senate Democratic incumbents. In 1984 and 1986, only about 20 percent of all Senate member-PAC money given to Democrats was given to incumbents. In 1988, when Robert Byrd of West Virginia stepped down as Senate majority leader, the PACs of Senators Daniel K. Inouye of Hawaii and J. Bennett Johnston of Louisiana actively contributed to Senate Democratic incumbents, boosting the percentage of incumbents receiving money to 58 percent. But that is still far short of the 76 percent of Senate Democratic contributions that outside PACs give to incumbents.

The unusually high percentage of contributions to Senate Democratic challengers in 1986 was due to a strenuous—successful—Democratic effort to recapture the Senate, where the Republicans had won control in the 1980 elections. The Republicans mounted a similar effort in 1988, while Democrats, predictably, used contributions in the same year to shore up their incumbents. Republican leadership PACs in 1982 and 1984 favored incumbents in their efforts to preserve the GOP margin in the Senate.

Because leadership PACs give more money to challengers, they actually promote competition. Thus, the evidence suggests that leadership PACs may be disposed to some risk taking by giving to challengers. The pattern in the House and Senate appears to be for the majority party's leadership PACs to use their funds to shore up incumbents and for the minority party to concentrate on funding challengers.

There are several plausible explanations for this tendency on the part of leadership PACs to be more generous to challengers than are outside PACs.

The first explanation is a tactical one associated with campaigns for leadership posts. The votes of incumbent colleagues in a leadership contest are often declared well in advance of the vote. Indeed, one of the devices used by candidates for party or committee posts is to line up impressive numbers of colleagues before even formally announcing. While the firmness of this support is often questionable, there is a tendency for incumbent members to commit themselves early. The number of declared holdouts is usually small. This magnifies the importance of those who *might* be elected—candidates for open seats and challengers—and makes them more inviting targets for contributions that might influence their vote should they win. This has the effect of expanding the leadership electorate.

A second explanation for the greater disposition of leadership PACs to give to nonincumbents is that the objectives of such PACs are only partly legislative. Outside PACs' objectives are virtually exclusively tied to gaining access to specific committees; targeting money on a known incumbent is more prudent than giving money to a nonincumbent whose ultimate committee assignment is unknown. Leadership PACs, in contrast, know that at the very least the new member will have a vote in the party's caucus, which confirms committee chairs and party leadership posts.

Third, a large percentage of this money goes to candidates in special elections because there is pressure to get money to candidates as quickly as possible, and leadership PACs can act quickly.

Finally, the money given out by leadership PACs is probably more discretionary than that of outside PACs. Outside PACs tend to be very conscious of their "batting average," and the claim that the PAC supported winners adds much luster to a PAC director's resume.

For a House member or senator who operates a PAC, supporting winners is only one of many goals. There is less riding on any single contribution, and greater speculation is encouraged. Giving nonessential money to a challenger whose chances are rated about even can pay a handsome dividend in the form of a new colleague who is in your debt even before taking office.

Although the evidence still is skimpy, covering only three election cycles, two categories of incumbent recipients appear to be consistently getting an increasing share of money.

The first is Senate Democratic incumbents, whose share of their chamber's Democratic PAC money rose from roughly 20 percent in 1984 to more than 57 percent in 1988. The status of the senators who are up for reelection affects these figures considerably. A senatorial class with a large number of members under vigorous challenge will produce an outpouring of colleague support. The race to succeed Byrd also influenced this trend and made it difficult to sort out short-run and long-run factors.

The other category of incumbents whose share of leadership PAC money has risen is House Republicans. The percentage of total leadership PAC money going to House Republicans is still a relatively small share of the chamber totals, 43 percent. That figure, however, could be expected to rise dramatically if Robert Michel of Illinois were to announce his retirement as minority leader and there were competition for his post.

It appears that, although PACs may give disproportionately to incumbents and, by this pattern of giving, depress electoral competition, leadership PACs are more evenhanded.

Is Leadership PAC Overhead Excessively High?

One argument against leadership PACs is not that they contribute too generously to candidates but that, in light of their income, they give too small a portion of their receipts. Outside contributors might well have reason to be concerned that money donated to a leadership PAC might end up going for family travel expenses or elaborate office space rather than to worthy candidates. In fact, there is little evidence that leadership PACs spend excessively on overhead. About 15 percent of all leadership PAC receipts are given out in contributions to candidates (see Appendix, Table 4), but that figure, currently $2,427,020, is distorted by two large ideological PACs that have overhead exceeding 20 percent: the Congressional Club, founded by Senator Jesse Helms of North Carolina, and Independent Action, established by Representative Morris Udall of Arizona and Senator Thomas Harkin of Iowa. When those two leadership PACs are excluded, contributions are 19 percent of receipts.

When the leadership PACs operated by members of Congress with declared presidential ambitions also are removed from the list, contributions as a percentage of receipts rise to almost 30 percent. This suggests that "pure" leadership PACs established by House members and senators without presidential plans give out a higher percentage of their income in contributions to candidates. And leadership PACs give out a higher percentage of receipts in campaign contributions than do a selected group of ten ideological outside PACs (see Appendix, Table 5). Leadership PACs, accordingly, do not devote an excessive portion of their receipts to overhead. From 1983 to 1988, contributions ranged from 25 percent to 30 percent of receipts.

Looking at all objections to leadership PACs, it is clear that the greatest damage is not inflicted on citizens or the process of democratic choice. The total amount of leadership PAC money is still small in comparison to total spending by all PACs. If leadership PAC money were withdrawn from the funds available to candidates, the effect would hardly be noticed.

It is in the internal affairs of Congress and the face that Congress, as an institution, displays to the world that leadership PACs may give rise to problems. They promote the creation of power centers that act as rivals to the party leadership. Leadership PAC contributions to colleagues, moreover, are not simply made to influence votes in leadership contests. They can also be used to influence legislation. As one former member put it, "They allow committee and subcommittee chairmen who have them [PACs] to build a kind of machine to get members obligated to them so that they are really not using their own judgment on the issue. The people who get the money feel obligated to go along with the persons who gave it." This kind of money just reduces the independence of the recipient. And as members who have the PAC multiply the number of people they give money to, it makes donors more independent of the leadership of Congress as an institution and makes it harder for the leaders to set the agenda of Congress.

Do Leadership PACs Contribute to an Unfavorable Image of Congress?

Leadership PACs are part of a larger image problem from which Congress suffers. The unfavorable view of Congress could be seen in the outcry against and eventual defeat of legislation in 1989 that would have raised the salaries of top-level federal officials—including members of Congress—by 50 percent.

The abolition of leadership PACs alone would probably not do much to burnish the image of Congress, but as part of a larger package of reform—such as the elimination of members' honoraria for outside speaking engagements—a more positive picture might be presented. Appearances in politics are important, and a citizen who observed a member of Congress making contributions to colleagues as part of a campaign for a leadership post might well conclude that the donation was part of a quid pro quo for votes. Although caucus votes on chairmanships are normally by secret ballot, the published FEC reports on contributions leave ample room for observers to make inferences about the matters of members of Congress who donate to their colleagues. Charles Bennett of Florida, defeated for chairmanship of the House Armed Services Committee by a colleague who gave liberally to committee members, put it this way:

> I don't think any member of Congress ever said, "Give me the money and I'll vote for you," or said, "You've given me the money and because of that I'll vote for you." But a hell of a lot of people around here say, "I'm very happy to receive the money and since you're running for chairman you can count on my vote." That [is] a very narrow line and I'm not sure that folks on the outside can find the distinction.

So while there is no clear evidence of vote buying with contributions from leadership PAC funds, it is difficult for the public to avoid concluding that there is a quid pro quo.

Chapter 5

Is Reform Possible?

It is not necessary to venture far into the arcane world of political campaign finance to realize how difficult it is to achieve incremental reform. Those who buy access easily foil reforms that are attractive, modest, and workable politically. Far-reaching reforms such as public financing of campaigns could purge the system of the distorting effects of money, but they are usually adjudged to be politically unrealistic.* So those who deplore the spectacle of elections that seem to go to the highest bidder are caught between the easily circumvented halfway measure on the one hand and the ideal and unachievable on the other.

The reef around which several efforts at reform must steer is the Supreme Court decision in *Buckley v. Valeo,* which invalidated limits on expenditures by House and Senate candidates. The Court held that the spending of money is tantamount to free speech. In desperation,

---

* A 1988 poll of eight hundred voters by the firm of Dressner, Sykes, Jordan, and Townsend for the New York State Commission on Government Integrity found that only 15 percent of the respondents favored public financing of campaigns while overwhelmingly being in favor of "reform" in the abstract.

some campaign finance reformers have suggested that Congress go ahead and pass another law limiting expenditures just to give the Court a chance to change its mind. Senator Ernest Hollings of South Carolina, in the 100th Congress, introduced S.J. Res. 282, a constitutional amendment to allow Congress to legislate spending limits. A Republican filibuster killed the proposed amendment on April 21, 1988.

Most efforts at campaign finance reform in the 100th Congress—of 1987 and 1988—dealt with the broader questions of campaign-finance reform rather than leadership PACs or member-to-member contributions. In general, the proposals attempt to get candidates to accept campaign expenditure limits in conjunction with voluntary participation in a public finance system. H.R. 2464, of which Al Swift, a Democrat from Washington, is the principal sponsor, and S. 2, of which David Boren, a Democrat from Oklahoma, is the principal sponsor, both take this approach. Morris Udall's H.R. 2473 laid down a challenge to the Court by imposing limits on spending without any link to a public finance scheme.

Three House bills in the 100th Congress addressed directly the question of leadership PACs and member-to-member contributions. The Swift bill, introduced in May 1987, contains the following provision: "A candidate for Federal office may not establish, maintain, or control a political committee, other than an authorized committee of the candidate or a committee of a political party."[1]

A month later, a bill co-sponsored by Tony Coelho, Jim Leach (a Republican from Iowa), and Mike Synar contained identical language. The latter bill also restricted the practice of *bundling*—when a PAC or individual assembles large numbers of checks from individuals to specific candidates to circumvent the contribution limitation imposed on them. The proposal would also make it more difficult for members to act as conduits for their colleagues, by asking outside contributors to give money to a colleague. While there is no written record when an intermediary encourages the contribution, the recipient is typically made aware of the author of his or her good fortune and is free to express gratitude to the patron's leadership race or in support of pet legislation.

A year after the introduction of the Coelho-Leach-Synar bill, Charles Bennett introduced H.R. 4918, which would ban all member-to-member contributions and prohibit the solicitation or acceptance of contributions for leadership races in the House.

Evaluating the Reform Proposals

Efforts at reforming campaign finance overall are not within the purview of this examination. The concern here is with the more specific question of the role members of Congress play in funding their colleagues' campaigns in return for support in leadership contests or on legislation.

The banning of leadership PACs in the Swift bill and the Coelho-Leach-Synar bill would leave intact the ability of members to contribute to colleagues out of their cash on hand. While banning of member PACs would reduce the amount that could be donated—because of the lower limits set on individual donations—individual member's campaign committees could still give $1,000 per election to members.

The Bennett bill, which addresses the problem more comprehensively, would eliminate all member-to-member contributions whether they originate in leadership PACs or in a member's campaign committee. The Bennett bill, however, does not tackle the problem of members acting as conduits for contributions.

The abolition of leadership PACs and restrictions on

the use of leftover campaign funds would not deal a mortal blow to the problems associated with the deluge of political money to modern campaigns, but would serve to cleanse, somewhat, the soul of Congress.

Members ought to care deeply about the institution even as some of them gain political credit with their constituents by damning it or by insinuating that they are not really part of the "mess in Washington." While imperfections in the broader political system may be beyond simple legislative solutions, members of Congress have considerable control over practices within Congress. They need to tend to the reality as well as the image: money is the pivot on which much in Congress turns.

However, the brokerage of outside money to colleagues is extremely difficult to regulate. It is a problem akin to that of forbidding the so-called independent expenditure committee from colluding with the campaigns whose activities they benefit but with which they cannot legally be affiliated. It might also be likened to the difficulty of enforcing insider-trading laws on Wall Street. Yet such laws are on the books. In the former case there has been little evidence of collusion, and to the latter case the stringent new penalties for insider trading have yet to have their effect. Clearly, no effort to curtail or eliminate leadership PACs or contributions by members to colleagues could succeed without antibrokering legislation.

But antibrokering legislation would complicate a practice that is not harmful—the practice of House members and senators assisting colleagues with fund-raising activities. This is a time-honored practice that builds interpersonal bonds among members and even strengthens party allegiance and consensus.

The Legislative Culture and the Limits of Reform

Addressing the problems associated with leadership PACs and the excesses of member-to-member contributions requires an appreciation of the subtle and important colleague relationships in Congress and their larger implications for the political system.

There is, in Congress, a well-established set of norms that stresses, among other things, friendly relations and reciprocity among colleagues. Both formal rules and informal folkways of the House and Senate serve to inhibit conflict and foster comity. The requirement that members be addressed by honorifics ("the Senator from —— or "the distinguished member from ——") makes it more difficult to inject rancor into debates. Similarly, most members believe in vote trading or reciprocity where a member will support a measure of benefit to a colleague's district in the expectation that the favor will be returned. Fund-raising on behalf of colleagues is part of this legislative culture of mutual accommodation and aid.

The appearance at a fund-raising event in a colleague's district is part of the currency of interpersonal relationships among members of Congress, but it has broader implications as well. The practice serves to nationalize politics and to reduce the parochialism that comes from a system in which "all politics is local," in the words of former Speaker O'Neill.

It would be unwise to interfere with the practice of fund-raising for colleagues. It builds solidarity and cohesion within the institution and in the political system in the broadest sense. An influential member of Congress would not even need to direct an outside contributor to support a colleague: that member's very presence at a fund-raiser would send a clear signal to guests.

To crack down on these practices with unenforceable regulations might be temporarily satisfying but would not accomplish much. There are, however, some useful measures that could at least alleviate the problems.

Four Reform Proposals

Ban Member PACs. Multicandidate campaign committees established by members of Congress introduce considerable distortion into the legislative process by fragmenting the authority of party leaders. In addition, PACs, with their ability to contribute up to $5,000, can influence the election of committee chairs and other leaders in a manner that can be perceived as improper by the media and by citizens.

The average size of a leadership PAC contribution in 1988 was almost $2,000. Donations of this size can have an effect, and the restriction of members to the $1,000 limit on individual contributions would seem to be enough to enable legislators to help colleagues or other candidates without appearing to be buying favor. In the case of leadership PACs, with their far higher limit per candidate per election, a cut to $1,000 would be perceived as a radical downward revision of the ceiling on donations. These contributions from principal campaign committees should not be banned.

The total amount of contributions from House and Senate incumbents' personal campaign funds to all congressional candidates came to only $495,250 for Democrats and Republicans in both houses as of September 30, 1988. Of this total, $314,530 went to Democrats and $180,720 to Republicans. This is less than half the total given out by leadership PACs. While the practice of making cash-on-hand contributions to colleagues is fairly widespread—about 35 percent of the members made them in 1988—the average contribution is much smaller than the average leadership PAC donation. With a maximum of $1,000 on contributions, the likelihood of abuse is small. If the more sweeping reforms advocated by Bennett were pursued—as they should be—the technique for dealing with these cash-on-hand contributions would be to require members to "zero out" the treasuries of their principal campaign committees at the end of each election cycle and return unused funds to contributors.

Policing How Campaign Funds Are Used. The amount of money passing between the campaign committees of members of Congress is less consequential than the way the money is used. The use of campaign funds to buy race track tickets for precinct workers for Dan Rostenkowski of Illinois or to pay a taxidermist to stuff and mount a mule deer for E. ("Kika") de la Garza of Texas seem to be dubious expenditures.

Some of these outlays are considerable. Henry Gonzalez of Texas, chairman of the House Banking Committee, paid out almost $3,500 to fly into Washington a mariachi band from San Antonio to play at his birthday party. Ways and Means Committee chairman Rostenkowski spent $43,000 from his campaign funds on meals and liquor at Chicago-area restaurants and country clubs.[2]

While congressional rules limit the uses to which campaign funds can be put, the rules need to be policed. Simple disclosure does not seem to deter these questionable expenditures.

Encourage Members to Establish Special-Interest Committees within Their Party's Campaign Committee. As one alternative to leadership PACs or member-to-member contributions, Senator Thomas Daschle of South Dakota in 1988 established the regional program of the Democratic Senate Campaign Committee. The program enables Democratic senators to provide additional support to Senate candidates from their own region.

Increase the Maximum that the Parties' Congressional Campaign Committees May Contribute to Their Candidates. This would increase the ability of party leaders to influence elections and enhance their stature and political leverage within the institution. The law treats party campaign committees differently from ordinary PACs. While party money in the aggregate is not trivial, the funds that party leaders have at their committees' disposal ought to be greater. The four congressional party campaign committees are limited to $10,000 per candidate in a single primary-election cycle. While national committee money and state money is also available to candidates, these amounts are drops in the bucket in House campaigns that can cost more than $1 million and Senate campaigns that can cost $10 million.

Increasing the contribution ceiling for the party campaign committees would make these committees bigger players in the PAC world and raise the influence of party money relative to other sources of contributions.

The Logistics of Reforming Leadership PACs

Although it may be desirable to eliminate member PACs, given the danger of fragmentation they pose, it is necessary to examine how they might be banned. The answer is not necessarily straightforward.

The legislation introduced in recent years to eliminate leadership PACs would be challenged rigorously even if it passed Congress. The obstacle is the Supreme Court decision in *Buckley v. Valeo.* A decision equating the spending of campaign money with freedom of speech is difficult to circumvent. There is no reason to think that the Court would approve an act of Congress that imposed free-speech limitations on House members and senators any more than it would approve such restrictions on ordinary citizens. The abolition of leadership PACs would mean negotiating that constitutional mine field. Does that mean leadership PACs cannot be limited or abolished?

The answer is that vehicles other than acts of Congress can achieve the same objective without running the risk of being struck down as unconstitutional. Interviews with staff members of the House Rules Committee and congressional parliamentarians suggest two alternative courses for reform in the House, where leadership PACs are most prevalent.

A Change in House Rules

This is the bipartisan approach to reform because it would abolish leadership PACs through the use of the standing committees of the House to modify House rules. Section 43 of the Code of Official Conduct would have to be modified. The code deals with such issues as gifts to members and prohibiting the use of campaign funds for personal purposes.

The House Committee on Standards of Official Conduct (known as the Ethics Committee) would have to hold hearings on leadership PACs and make recommendations to the Rules Committee, which would then hold hearings on these recommendations.

Normally such modifications to House rules are not "privileged"— requiring an "order-of-business" rule before the substance of the reform resolution could be debated. It is an extra step that the House imposes in its internal legislative process. Accordingly, the House could defeat the reform measure simply by voting against the order-of-business rules and without debating the merits of the resolution itself.

The only time when such rule changes do not require the order-of-business rule is on the opening day of Congress every two years. This is known as House Resolution 5, which readopts the rules of the previous Congress along with any changes or new rules.

Using this process would involve Democratic and Republican support and would give the rules change bipartisan legitimacy. On the other hand, it is usually difficult to build up bipartisan consensus on matters relating to campaign-finance reform. As for the constitutionality problem that would afflict a change in the law—the other reform route—one Rules Committee staff member commented, "No court in the land would strike down a House rule as unconstitutional."

A Change in Caucus Rules

When the majority party in Congress changes the rules of its own caucus and they become binding on its members, it is often tantamount to a change in the formal rules of the chamber. Many of the major reforms of the 1960s and 1970s were merely changes in Democratic Caucus rules rather than House rules changes. Two factors argue for the use of change in Democratic Caucus rules to effect the reform of leadership PACs.

The first is that the Democrats are the majority party in the House and are likely to be the dominant party for the near future. One-third—seventeen—of the leadership PACs in the House and Senate, moreover, were established by House Democrats, so a caucus rule change for Democrats disallowing such PACs would have considerable impact.

Second, the House Democratic Caucus has a more formal and firmly established set of rules than does the Republican House Conference. The ground rules for the conference are a series of resolutions. The more canonical quality of the Democratic Caucus rules would be more likely to entrench this reform.

Initiating a caucus rules change for House Democrats begins with the Committee on Organization Study and Review of the House Democratic Caucus that could propose the abolition of leadership PACs. Sample wording might be: "It shall be the policy of the Democratic Caucus that no member shall form a political action committee for the purpose of making contributions to any other member of Congress or candidate for Congress."

If the Committee on Organization Study and Review approved the change, it would then be recommended to the organizing caucus of the Democrats that meets in the December preceding the January convening of the new Congress. The change would be debated in the caucus and if approved would be included in the House rules changes in House Resolution 5. This resolution is usually adopted on a straight party-line vote and would be adopted if Democrats were in the majority.

The use of the caucus rule change rather than the House rules change involves a trade-off between the higher likelihood of a consensus in an exclusively Democratic gathering versus the greater legitimacy that would come as the result of bipartisan action. Either route, however, is preferable to a change of federal law because of the constitutionality problem.

Leadership PACs: Praise by Faint Damnation

If after intensive examination of a problem, a conclusion is drawn that it may be less vexatious than originally believed, the problem is not converted into a virtue. Leadership PACs and member-to-member contributions are part of the larger danger of the excessive reliance of U.S. politics on money. Although each aspect of the problem may, by itself, have little impact, the cumulative effect can be significant. What can be said of this one part?

First, there is little evidence of trickery or misrepresentation in the dealings of member PACs with

habitual contributors such as outside PACs and peren-
nial givers. There is, also, little evidence that the overhead costs of leadership PACs are excessive or that
money is not being recycled to candidates. Habitual
donors seem resigned to having at least part of their contributions end up in hands that they would not have
given to directly. However, occasional individual givers
might well be misled into thinking that money given
to a leadership PAC will end up only with recipients of
whom they would approve.

Second, the goals of leadership PACs and party campaign committees evidently do not differ significantly.
The lists of recipients from the two sets of contributors
are similar. Indeed, members who have their own PACs
may even comply with requests from party leaders to
contribute to specified candidates. Still, the decision to
establish leadership PACs is not made primarily with
party goals in mind but to foster the goals of the founder. Although the recipients of funds from the party's
campaign committees and the PACs operated by members may be largely the same, the present system is an
inefficient way of getting money to candidates.

Third, the leadership PACs are *less* pro-incumbent
than outside PACs. And the policies of individual members in doling out cash from their own campaign committees to candidates may even be more prochallenger
than those of leadership PACs. Clyde Wilcox found that
members' campaign committees gave only about 52 percent of their money to incumbents.[3]

In one way, leadership PACs may *help* the parties. The
money that might be freed up by abolishing leadership
PACs would not necessarily find its way into party
coffers. The PACs thus bring in more money to party candidates. Those who give money to leadership PACs do
so to win points with individual legislators and may even
consider donations to party committees unproductive of
their legislative aims.

* * *

The general conclusion, though, is that leadership PACs, especially if they continue to proliferate, will magnify the influence of individual members. The greater the number of important players armed with their own checkbooks, the harder the job of party leaders as they try to manage the delicate and often frustrating task of building parliamentary majorities. The result is an increasing fragmentation of power and decreasing importance of parties, the basis of our form of democracy.

PACs not only pose a threat to the traditional party structure of our government, they also contribute to the growing perception of a political system run by money—a system that is, if not corrupt, corruptible. This negative perception played a role in the strong, adverse public response to the question of a pay raise for Congress.

It is no surprise that Americans—barraged by stories of individual corruption, huge amounts of funds being used to buy votes from fellow lawmakers, and excessive honoraria and junkets—have come to believe that politicians seek personal enrichment at the expense of the citizenry. Such stories make it all too easy to forget the problems created by the need for money to finance increasingly expensive campaigns. Thus, even though leadership PACs did not cause the parties' problems nor bring about this disillusionment with politicians, they exacerbate the problems—and they will continue to do so unless changes are made.

Appendix

Table 1
Report on All PAC Activity for 1984-88[a] (figures in $)

	1984	1986	1988
Total Contributions to			
Congressional Candidates[b]	111,450,482	139,770,157	91,883,827
Democrats	63,063,744	78,835,514	59,619,854
	(56.6%)	(56.4%)	(64.9%)
Republicans	48,361,505	60,919,350	32,243,220
	(43.4%)	(43.6%)	(35.1%)
Breakdown of Contributions	*(in percentage terms)*		
Democrats			
Senate Incumbents	51.4	42.9	75.9
Senate Challengers	29.9	35.7	13.2
Senate Open-Seat Candidates	18.7	21.4	10.9
	100.0	100.0	100.0
House Incumbents	82.0	75.1	87.5
House Challengers	11.0	12.2	7.7
House Open-Seat Candidates	7.0	12.7	4.8
	100.0	100.0	100.0

Table 1 (continued)

Republicans			
Senate Incumbents	76.8	67.8	76.4
Senate Challengers	9.6	8.3	12.5
Senate Open-Seat Candidates	13.6	23.9	11.1
	100.0	100.0	100.0
House Incumbents	65.4	76.8	92.2
House Challengers	21.5	7.6	2.9
House Open-Seat Candidates	13.1	15.6	4.9
	100.0	100.0	100.0
Contributions Overall			
To Incumbents	72.3	68.8	84.4
To Challengers	16.3	14.2	8.6
To Open-Seat Candidates	11.4	17.0	7.0
	100.0	100.0	100.0

a. 1988 figures are through June 30.
b. Includes candidates not running in the 1986 cycle.

Table 2

Leadership PACs of Incumbent Senators and House Members as Registered with the Federal Election Commission, October 1988

Individual	Party/State	Office Held	PAC Name or Title
Rudy Boschwitz	R-Minn.	Senate	Plaid PAC
Robert C. Byrd	D-W.Va.	Senate	Committee for America's Future
William L. Clay	D-Mo.	House	Congressional Black Caucus PAC
Thad Cochran	R-Miss.	Senate	Senate Victory Fund PAC
Tony Coelho	D-Calif.	House	Valley Education Fund
Kent Conrad	D-N.Dak.	Senate	Fund for New Leadership
Jim Courter	R-N.J.	House	Fund for Responsible Leadership
Philip M. Crane	R-Ill.	House	Americans for a Constitutional Congress
Alan Cranston	D-Calif.	Senate	Committee for a Democratic Consensus
John C. Danforth	R-Mo.	Senate	Fund for the Future Committee
Dennis DeConcini	D-Ariz.	Senate	Arizona Leadership for America Search Committee
Robert K. Dornan	R-Calif.	House	American Space Frontier Committee, American Citizens for Political Action
David Dreier	R-Calif.	House	97th Club Campaign Committee, California Congress, Republican PAC
Ronnie G. Flippo	D-Ala.	House	Responsible Government Fund
Thomas S. Foley	D-Wash.	House	House Leadership Fund

Table 2 (continued)

Richard A. Gephardt	D-Mo.	House	Effective Government Fund
Newt Gingrich	R-Ga.	House	Conservative Opportunity Society PAC
John Glenn	D-Ohio	Senate	National Council on Public Policy
Phil Gramm	R-Tex.	Senate	Conservative Democratic PAC; "Boll Weevil PAC" [a]
William H. Gray III	D-Pa.	House	Committee for Democratic Opportunity
Bill Green	R-N.Y.	House	Modern PAC
Jesse A. Helms	R-N.C.	Senate	National Congressional Club
Ernest F. Hollings	D-S.C.	Senate	Citizens for a Competitive America
Daniel K. Inouye	D-Hawaii	Senate	Senate Majority Fund
J. Bennett Johnston	D-La.	Senate	Pelican PAC
Edward M. Kennedy	D-Mass.	Senate	Fund for a Democratic Majority
Frank R. Lautenberg	D-N.J.	Senate	Campaign for America
Marvin Leath	D-Tex.	House	Committee for a Democratic Consensus
Bill Lowery	R-Calif.	House	American Enterprise PAC
Richard G. Lugar	R-Ind.	Senate	Republican Majority Fund
Edward R. Madigan	R-Ill.	House	15th District Committee
Edward J. Markey	D-Mass.	House	U.S. Committee Against Nuclear War; Nat'l Committee for Peace in Central America
James A. McClure	R-Idaho	Senate	Leadership USA
Robert H. Michel	R-Ill.	House	Republican Leaders Fund

Table 2 (continued)

Mary Rose Oakar	D-Ohio	House	Economic Security PAC
David R. Obey	D-Wis.	House	Committee for a Progressive Congress
Claude D. Pepper	D-Fla.	House	Senior PAC
Charles B. Rangel	D-N.Y.	House	Committee for the 100th Congress
Dan Rostenkowski	D-Ill.	House	America's Leaders Fund
Paul Simon	D-Ill.	Senate	Democracy Fund [b]
Charles W. Stenholm	D-Tex.	House	Conservative Democratic PAC
Ted Stevens	R-Alaska	Senate	Fund for a Republican Majority
William M. Thomas	R-Calif.	House	96th Club Campaign Committee
Strom Thurmond	R-S.C.	Senate	Americans for Good Government
Morris K. Udall and Tom Harkin	D-Ariz. D-Iowa	House Senate	Independent Action
Henry A. Waxman	D-Calif.	House	24th Congressional District of California PAC
Lowell P. Weicker	R-Conn.	Senate	Senate Constitutional Federal PAC
Pete Wilson	R-Calif.	Senate	California for America
James C. Wright	D-Tex.	House	Majority Congress Committee Fund for New Leadership

a. This PAC was established while Gramm was still a Democrat and still in the House.
b. Used primarily for 1988 Democratic presidential primaries.
Source: Federal Election Commission

Table 3
Leadership PAC Activity in 1984, 1986, and 1988[a]

Contributions to House Candidates ($)

	Total	Democrats	Republicans	All Incumbents	Democratic Incumbents	Republican Incumbents
1984	1,101,657	578,401	502,756	543,767	374,361	151,401
(% of total)[b]	—	(52.5)	(48.5)	(49.4)	(64.7)	(30.1)
1986	2,292,371	1,929,717	357,154	1,046,696	935,897	95,049
(% of total)	—	(84.1)	(15.9)	(45.6)	(48.5)	(26.6)
1988	605,706	553,520	51,500	328,550	306,781	24,769
(% of total)	—	(91.4)	(8.6)	(54.2)	(55.4)	(48.0)

(continued on next page)

Table 3 (continued)

Contributions to Senate Candidates ($)

	Total	Democrats	Republicans	All Incumbents	Democratic Incumbents	Republican Incumbents
1984	870,725	157,752	704,642	464,276	31,289	432,987
(% of total)[b]	—	(17.7)	(82.3)	(46.7)	(20.2)	(61.4)
1986	1,421,888	667,017	731,493	520,352	148,610	371,742
(% of total)	—	(47.0)	(53.0)	(45.8)	(22.3)	(50.8)
1988	406,082	257,946	148,316	243,031	144,940	98,091
(% of total)	—	(63.5)	(36.5)	(59.8)	(56.2)	(66.2)

a. 1988 figures are through June 30.
b. Percentages for Democratic and Republican incumbents represent the portion of all Democratic and Republican contributions, respectively, going to incumbents.

Table 4
Leadership PAC Contributions as a Percentage of Receipts

All Leadership PACs Studied

Cycle	Receipts ($)	Contributions ($)	Contributions as percentage of receipts
1977-78	317,430	62,485	19.7
1979-80	8,599,123	206,585	2.4
1981-82	15,973,330	1,176,506	7.4
1983-84	19,973,330	1,916,882	10.0
1985-86	34,620,790	3,651,717	6.2
1987-88[a]	15,725,053	2,427,020	15.4

Excluding Ideological Leadership PACs[b]

1977-78	317,430	62,485	19.7
1979-80	725,149	134,204	18.5
1981-82	5,037,376	931,403	18.5
1983-84	12,497,218	1,717,057	13.3
1985-86	17,126,297	3,384,407	19.8
1987-88[a]	11,363,369	2,265,942	19.4

Table 4 (continued)

Excluding Ideological and Presidential Leadership PACs[c]

Cycle	Receipts ($)	Contributions ($)	Contributions as percentage of receipts
1977-78	72,850	42,950	59.0
1979-80	208,130	132,204	63.5
1981-82	1,584,886	669,593	42.2
1983-84	4,236,724	1,095,362	25.9
1985-86	12,313,012	2,837,149	23.0
1987-88[a]	6,550,084	1,754,927	29.8

a. 1988 cycle figures are current to October 20, 1988.

b. PACs excluded: National Congressional Club, Independent Action.

c. PACs excluded: National Congressional Club, Independent Action, Campaign America, Campaign for Prosperity, Citizens for a Competitive America, Democracy Fund, Effective Government Fund, Fund for '86, National Council on Public Policy.

Table 5
Contributions as a Percentage of Receipts
for Selected Ideological Outside PACs[a]

Cycle	Receipts ($)	Contributions ($)	Contributions as percentage of receipts
1977-78	4,419,661	749,022	16.9
1979-80	6,980,769	1,062,812	15.2
1981-82	10,551,487	1,541,285	14.6
1983-84	12,549,767	1,759,769	14.0
1985-86	8,665,624	1,772,426	20.5
1987-88[b]	6,603,193	1,380,568	20.9

a. PACs included: Americans for Democratic Action, Committee for America's Future, Conservative Victory Fund, Democrats for the '80s, DSG Campaign Fund, Free Congress PAC, Fund for a Conservative Majority, Hollywood Women's PAC, National Committee for an Effective Congress, Republican Boosters Club.
b. 1988 cycle figures are current to October 20, 1988.

Notes

Introduction

1. Bob Benenson, *Congressional Quarterly*, August 2, 1986.

2. Norman J. Ornstein et al., *Vital Statistics on Congress* (Washington, D.C.: American Enterprise Institute, 1984), pp. 112-13.

Chapter 1

1. Irving R. Kaufman, "Electoral Integrity vs. Free Speech," *New York Times*, March 7, 1988.

2. Dexter Filkins, "The Only Issue Is Money," *Washington Post*, National Weekly Edition, June 13-19, 1988.

3. *Congress Speaks—A Survey of the 100th Congress* (Washington, D.C.: Center for Responsive Politics, 1988), pp. 90-93.

4. Mike Synar, "Campaign Financing and the Need for Reform," *Extensions*, Winter 1988, p. 21; and Frank J. Sorauf, *Money in American Elections* (Glenview, Ill.: Scott, Foresman, 1988), pp. 54-55.

5. Larry J. Sabato, *PAC Power* (New York: W. W. Norton, 1985), pp. 152-59.

6. Stephen A. Salmore and Barbara G. Salmore, *Candidates, Parties and Campaigns* (Washington, D.C.: Congressional Quarterly Press, 1985), p. 234.

7. Ibid.

Chapter 2

1. Robert A. Caro, *The Years of Lyndon Johnson: The Path to Power* (New York: Knopf, 1982), pp. 606-36.

2. Ibid., p. 659.

3. Ibid., p. 663.

4. Ibid.

5. Thomas P. O'Neill, *Man of the House* (New York: Random House, 1988), pp. 154-55.

6. Ibid., pp. 207-8.

7. Robert L. Peabody, ed., *Leadership in Congress* (Boston: Little, Brown, 1976), p. 39.

8. Ibid., p. 262.

9. Gary C. Jacobson, *The Politics of Congressional Elections* (Boston: Little, Brown, 1987), p. 69.

10. Ibid., p. 63.

11. Janet Hook, "House Leadership Races Turn into Marathon," *Congressional Quarterly Weekly Report,* November 14, 1987, pp. 2801-2.

12. Peabody, *Leadership in Congress,* pp. 249-50.

13. Thomas P. Southwick, "House Leadership Race: Wide Open Contest," *Congressional Quaterly Weekly Report,* October 9, 1976, pp. 2895-2900.

14. See Barbara G. Salmore and Stephen A. Salmore, "Back to Basics: Party as Legislative Caucus" (Unpublished manuscript, Eagleton Institute of Politics, Rutgers University, 1988).

Chapter 3

1. Steven Waldman, "The Hiroshima Hustle," *Washington Monthly,* October 1986, pp. 35-40.

2. Ibid.

3. Ibid.

4. Dana Bottorff, "California's Congressional Delegation Moves Center Stage," *California Journal,* August 1986, p. 379.

5. Bob Benenson, "In the Struggle for Influence, Members' PACs Gain Ground," *Congressional Quarterly Weekly Report,* August 2, 1986, p. 1751.

6. Ibid.

7. "Winning Elections and Influencing Friends," *Campaign Industry News,* April 1988.

8. Shannon Bradley, "Oakar Claims Lead in Dems' Caucus Race," *Roll Call*, November 29, 1987.

9. Shannon Bradley, "Forget Iowa: The Really Heavy Campaigning Is in West Virginia, for Chair of the Democratic Caucus," *Roll Call*, February 7, 1988.

10. "Winning Elections and Influencing Friends."

11. Shannon Bradley, "Attending Gray Dinner Nets Members $1,000," *Roll Call*, February 28, 1988.

12. Ibid.

13. Shannon Bradley, "Gray Asks Donors to Fund Caucus Race," *Roll Call*, May 22, 1988.

14. Shannon Bradley, "Lobbyists Are Recruited to Solicit Members' Support in House Democratic Race," *Roll Call*, June 12, 1988.

Chapter 4

1. Clyde Wilcox, "Share the Wealth: Contributions by Congressional Incumbents to the Campaigns of Other Candidates," Paper presented at the 1988 meeting of the American Political Science Association, Washington, D.C., September 1988, pp. 10-11.

2. Brooks Jackson, *Honest Graft* (New York: Knopf, 1988), p. 288.

3. Nelson Polsby, "Two Strategies of Influence: Choosing a Majority Leader, 1962," in *Leadership in Congress*, ed. Robert L. Peabody (Boston: Little, Brown, 1976), pp. 66-99.

4. Philip M. Stern, *The Best Congress Money Can Buy* (New York: Pantheon, 1988), pp. 36-37.

5. Frank J. Sorauf, *Money in American Elections* (Glenview, Ill.: Scott, Foresman, 1988), p. 103.

Chapter 5

1. U.S. Congress, House, "Amendments to the Federal Election Campaign Act of 1971," 100th Cong., 1st sess., May 19, 1987, H.R. 2464, sec. 105.

2. Kenneth R. Weiss, "Critics Say Election Spending Goes Too Far," *New York Times*, November 6, 1988.

3. Wilcox, "Share the Wealth," p. 18.

Index